The Conscious Kitchen

I'd like to thank my husband for supporting me and believing in every single project I've undertaken. My sister, for her constant humor and invaluable input and for always humbling me. And my community, for the support they've shown me over the years while I've grown into a more informed and well-rounded creator. I hope I've done you justice.

Quarto.com

© 2024 Quarto Publishing Group USA Inc.

Text © 2024 Imogen Lucas

First Published in 2024 by Fair Winds Press,
an imprint of The Quarto Group,
100 Cummings Center, Suite 265-D
Beverly, MA 01915, USA.
T (978) 282-9590
F (978) 283-2742

Fair Winds Press titles are also available at discount for retail, wholesale, promotional, and bulk purchase. For details, contact the Special Sales Manager by email at specialsales@quarto.com or by mail at The Quarto Group, Attn: Special Sales Manager, 100 Cummings Center, Suite 265-D, Beverly, MA 01915, USA.

28 27 26 25 24   1 2 3 4 5

ISBN: 978-0-7603-9022-1

Digital edition published in 2024
eISBN: 978-0-7603-9023-8

Library of Congress Cataloging-in-Publication Data

Names: Lucas, Immy, author.
Title: The conscious kitchen : a beginner's guide to creating a
    sustainable, no-waste kitchen for a healthier home and planet /
    Immy Lucas.
Description: Beverly, MA, USA : Fair Winds Press, an imprint of The
    Quarto Group, 2024. | Includes index. | Includes bibliographical
    references and index.
Identifiers: LCCN 2024012549 (print) | LCCN 2024012550 (ebook) |
    ISBN 9780760390221 (hardcover) | ISBN 9780760390238 (ebook)
Subjects: LCSH: Seasonal cooking. | Food waste--Prevention. | Food
    conservation. | LCGFT: Cookbooks.
Classification: LCC TX714 .L033 2024 (print) | LCC TX714 (ebook) |
    DDC 641.5/64--dc23/eng/20240410
LC record available at https://lccn.loc.gov/2024012549
LC ebook record available at https://lccn.loc.gov/202

Design: Tanya Jacobson, tanyajacobson.co
Page layout: The Quarto Group
Food stylist: Sheila Jarnes
Photography: Zack Bowen

Printed in China

The Conscious Kitchen

A Beginner's Guide to Creating a Sustainable,
No-Waste Kitchen for a Healthier Home and Planet

Immy Lucas

FAIR WINDS

Contents

Introduction

Every climate-conscious person I've met remembers the moment it clicked for them—the thing that made them realize they wanted to live a more sustainable lifestyle. It might have been watching a documentary on plant-based eating, or visiting a glacier that was actively melting, or simply noticing the amount of waste on our beaches and in our waterways. Whatever it was, it motivated them to want to make changes to their lifestyles to make them more sustainable and to make positive changes for the planet.

Many creative, industrious, and inventive people are working hard to ensure our future is bright. But where do we fit in? Where might we, as individuals, start? What can we do in our everyday lives to do our part and help contribute to a more sustainable world? Well, I think we should start with food.

I have always been very vocal about my love of food. I have been singing the praises of seasonal eating, shopping locally, and experimenting in the kitchen for many years, creating both long- and short-form content on YouTube and Instagram to encourage others to explore the world of food through the lens of sustainability. It has become my conscious kitchen—my mission to present the concepts of eating sustainably to as many people as possible, and I do it with the same enthusiasm that I bring to every new recipe I try.

So, what exactly is a conscious kitchen? Well, it involves eating seasonally, shopping locally where possible, and experimenting in the kitchen to reduce waste and get the most out of our food. While my conscious kitchen may be vegan, yours doesn't have to be. This book is aimed at helping you make better choices all around and hopefully beginning to incorporate more veggie-centric meals into your diet. Seasonal eating involves choosing fruits and vegetables that are at their peak freshness and flavor according to the current season. This practice

supports local farming and reduces the carbon footprint associated with transporting food long distances. Shopping locally complements this by purchasing food from nearby producers, which also supports the local economy and ensures fresher produce.

Experimenting in the kitchen means trying out new recipes, ingredients, and cooking techniques. It's about being creative with food preparation, exploring different cuisines, and perhaps developing a unique cooking style. This can lead to discovering new favorite dishes and a greater appreciation for the variety and possibilities of our food. Experimentation encourages learning and adaptability in cooking, making it a more enjoyable and personalized experience.

Over the years, the sustainable lifestyle has evolved in a wonderfully diverse way to truly exemplify what an eco-conscious life could be like. We've seen the "trash jar," the infamous symbol of living a zero-waste lifestyle (which isn't possible, by the way, so if you've been trying and haven't managed it, feel free to stop beating yourself up). We've seen plastic-free, raw vegan, low-waste, and low-impact (essentially another term for living a lifestyle that has minimal impact). The list goes on. What I've personally discovered is that this isn't a one-size-fits-all lifestyle and, therefore, we shouldn't create a solution that is intended for only one group of people. Instead, ideas shared here can be built upon, altered, or tailored to your situation, so you can design a conscious kitchen that works for you.

This book aims to offer you an insight into how to maintain a conscious kitchen because the things we eat, the foods we buy, and the waste we inevitably produce are a great place to start. We don't need to make huge changes immediately and overhaul every aspect of our lives. Instead, we can start small, experiment and explore, learn as we go, and grow outward once we have some fundamental pillars in place. The sustainability movement has changed quite dramatically over the past decade, and I'm hoping that we've reached a point where everyone feels like there is space for them. Now is the time to work together and build community.

After all, one of the best things about making YouTube videos and building a thoughtful community is the constant feedback loop. This community shared its knowledge with me about things such as accessibility, the impact of plastic in medical care, and the sparseness of public transportation across the country. I've made this education my base and did more research so I could turn out informed, accessible content so that others also could learn sustainable ways. I went from promoting the trash jar to asking people to write to their local legislators. From asking people to only shop at zero-waste stores to helping educate people on the different areas of composting and how to use veggie scraps in thoughtful ways.

In 2020, I started to focus in on food as the jumping-off point for a sustainable lifestyle. In many ways, food sits at the center of a sustainability intersection. I discovered that we cannot talk about sustainable coffee preparation methods without talking about ethical sourcing and certifications such as fair trade. Nor can we use spices such as cinnamon, nutmeg, and saffron without expanding on their long and storied history.

Establishing my conscious kitchen became my response to the growing food waste problem. Although the issue seems far beyond our cupboards and waste bins, we can do so many things to minimize waste in our homes and fight against the devaluing of one of our greatest resources. With

more research came more questions. Where do you think the greatest amount of food waste is produced in the US? On farms? In restaurants? In manufacturing? At supermarkets and retail stores? The answer may surprise you. According to ReFED, a national nonprofit dedicated to ending food loss, it's households that account for the largest proportion of food waste out of all sectors.

In fact, households waste significantly more than supermarkets. In 2021, US households wasted 44.1 million tons compared with the 5.12 million tons wasted by supermarkets. On a global scale, the Intergovernmental Panel on Climate Change (IPCC) estimates that food waste releases up to 10 percent of greenhouse gas emissions. These are pretty shocking statistics, but there is a good point to be drawn from them. If food waste is a significant contributor to climate change and most of it comes from our homes, this is something we have the power to change.

But food waste is just one area that we can address in our kitchens. The global food system faces huge challenges, not just in terms of the environment but also in relation to human rights and exploitation, economic inequality, social (in)justice, and the lack of resilience in the system itself. These issues are inextricably connected to deforestation, water pollution, soil degradation, and loss of biodiversity resulting from food production. While we can't single-handedly tackle these challenges—and while they are worth mentioning but are ultimately outside the scope of this book—by developing sustainable and ethical food practices such as sourcing locally, eating seasonally, buying in bulk where appropriate, and preparing food from scratch, we can do *something*.

How to Use This Book

It's a real privilege to have the time to learn, and so I feel it is my responsibility to help share these findings with as many people as possible. This mission informs every piece of content I create and will be shared with you in this book. So, let's take a look at what you can expect to learn.

This book is a comprehensive guide designed to transform the way you think about, purchase, consume, store, make, preserve, and dispose of food in your home kitchen. Whether you've dabbled in some of this before or you're just starting out, this book is aimed at empowering you with the knowledge and practical skills needed to make a positive impact in your kitchen and community. I'll walk you through food strategies, tips, and tricks so you don't feel overwhelmed and can seamlessly incorporate the conscious kitchen mission into your daily life. You'll learn to understand the importance of eating seasonally and locally, what the ethical considerations of certain foods such as coffee and chocolate are, and the role of zero-waste stores.

We'll explore effective strategies for reducing food and plastic waste, how to shop sustainably, and how to store food properly. We'll take a close look at various methods of food preservation, including fermenting, pickling, canning, freezing, dehydrating, and more, along with a collection of practical and waste-curbing recipes. Each chapter, organized by season, offers up delicious recipes using and preserving ingredients in that time period. Lastly, we'll cover several ways to use food waste, from scrap cooking to different techniques for composting, including vermicompost, the bokashi method, and hot compost.

As an aside, it should be noted that the recipes in this book are plant-based. The reason I focus on plant-based recipes is because of the growing research that eating fewer animal products is potentially kinder on our planet. Research suggests that a plant-based diet could significantly benefit the environment by reducing greenhouse gas emissions, land use, and water consumption associated with livestock farming. Livestock production is one of the major contributors to environmental issues, including deforestation, biodiversity loss, and methane emissions—a potent greenhouse gas. By shifting toward a diet with fewer animal products, you can lower your carbon footprint, conserve natural resources, and promote a more sustainable food system that is less taxing on the planet's ecosystems.

A final note before we dive in: The goal of the conscious kitchen is progress, not perfection. I fully realize that most people are not going to be able to source locally produced organic foods for everything or cook all their meals from scratch. And that's okay. Beating yourself up for failing to achieve "perfection" helps no one, although I understand the instinct. Rather, the goal here is to do what you can according to your individual circumstances and values. I've found that I can achieve much more when my actions are motivated by kindness rather than guilt. One of the keys to this, I have found, is flexibility. Let me give you an example.

One of the pillars of this book is to teach you how to take almost any recipe and adapt it to your preferences, ability, and what you have available. In other words, to develop a flexible approach. I remember fine-tuning the recipe for my first loaf of bread: finding the right rise time, learning how to fold it in just the right way to create a beautifully charred ear, and figuring out how to get the height I wanted. I had dabbled in sourdough for a while, and, although it produced great results, I wanted something that took less than 5 minutes to prepare. This is when I discovered no-knead bread. It worked perfectly for me, as someone who wants to make bread from scratch, but without devoting a huge amount of time to the endeavor. In this instance, flexibility opened the door to regular bread baking in my home. Is it as glorious as those perfectly kneaded sourdough loaves? No. But it *works*.

This approach also comes in handy when adapting recipes for the seasons. Maybe in the winter you'll use dried rosemary and sea salt, but in the fall, you'll use fresh figs and walnuts. Learning to adapt is one of the greatest skills I acquired on my scratch cooking journey.

CHAPTER

1

SOURCING, SEASONALITY, AND SUSTAINABILITY

As you read this book, remember to take on board what appeals to you, adapt it, make it your own, and leave the rest. I hope that you will view this book as both a guide and a movement toward a more conscious and sustainable way of living. Whether you're a novice in the kitchen or a seasoned cook, *The Conscious Kitchen* will offer you a new perspective on food and its impact on our world. Before you can create a conscious kitchen, you first need to understand the bigger world of food—how the food system got this way, why it is flawed, and why it's so important to learn how to source your food, shop seasonally, and do your best to prevent waste. Being a conscious cook and creating a conscious kitchen actually starts with how, when, and where we source our food. As individuals, we can take steps both big and small when it comes to sourcing our food that have positive impacts on the world. So, let's take a quick look back on the history of the food system so we can step consciously into the future.

The Global Food System

The impact of globalization on our food system has been profound. The US has access to a huge variety of foods, often flown from thousands of miles away, year-round. As consumers, we have become accustomed to the availability of blueberries in winter and sweet potatoes in summer.

It is a vast, interconnected, and dynamic system, but it is fragile. This has been brought sharply into focus in recent years as world events such as the COVID-19 pandemic and war in Ukraine have highlighted this food system's lack of resilience. One of its areas of weakness is a lack of diversity. Although the US diet is more diverse than ever before, on a global scale, our eating habits are more homogenous. The majority of the food we eat comes from a handful of plants—wheat, rice, soy, and maize, according to *The Changing Global Diet* by Sara Kammlade et al. (Palmira, Columbia: International Center for Tropical Agriculture, 2017). And only a small number of countries export the vast proportion of this produce—and we are more reliant than ever on food imported from abroad.

This is why the war in Ukraine directly contributed to famine in Somalia, which imported 100 percent of its wheat from Ukraine. It's also why extreme weather events don't just have an impact on the local level but also contribute to global food insecurity and volatile pricing. We also see a lack of diversity in the fact that a small number of large corporations control integral strands of the food system, such as grain trade, farm machinery, and agricultural chemicals. We see the same issue in supermarkets and the dominance of just a few retailers.

A lack of diversity is just one element of the global food system that compromises its resilience. It is beyond the scope of this book to explore the other elements, but the take-home message is this: When a food system that lacks resilience is faced with stressors, the inevitable consequences range from food insecurity to famine. According to a UNICEF report, 122 million more people in the world went hungry in 2022 than they did in 2019. This was not due to a lack of food produced but rather a complex web of factors, including poverty, conflict, and climate change. There is no doubt that if people are going hungry in a world where there is enough food, the system is broken.

How Supermarkets Changed Food Sourcing

We cannot talk about global food systems without first talking about how the supermarket came to dominate the food retail sector. Supermarkets are a relatively modern invention. Before they existed, grocery shopping in the global north looked very different; a customer might have to visit multiple different stores, such as the greengrocer, butcher, fishmonger, and dry goods store, to do their weekly shopping. Customers didn't just take items off the shelf; they would have to go up to the counter and an assistant would weigh and prepare the items according to how much was required.

Although this style of grocery shopping afforded opportunities for social interaction and customers could purchase exactly the quantities of goods they needed, it was a laborious process to have the assistants weigh and measure every single item. Prices also were relatively high because small grocery stores could sell only small quantities of items, and the personalized service from the assistants was expensive.

In 1916, everything changed. Piggly Wiggly, a grocery store like no other, opened in Memphis, Tennessee. For the first time, customers were expected to help themselves. It seems wild to imagine how revolutionary the idea of self-service stores was at the time, but it paved the way for what we recognize today as the modern supermarket.

The self-service model was a huge success. Not only did many more Piggly Wiggly stores pop up, but other grocery stores followed suit. But it wasn't until the opening of King Kullen in Queens, New York, in 1930, that the first true supermarket was born, embodying the philosophy of "pile 'em high, sell 'em cheap." With the US in the grip of the Great Depression, lower prices were more attractive than ever.

It wasn't just the introduction of the supermarket as a concept that fundamentally changed how US consumers did their shopping. The shopping cart was invented in the late 1930s, so customers were no longer limited by what they could carry in their basket. The fridge/freezer also became widely available, which meant that people could drive to the supermarket with its enormous parking lot, load up their carts with goods, and stock their fridge/freezer with more. Now that everything was on display for the customer, the supermarket implicitly encouraged the impulse purchase. Despite the economic downturn, the ground had been laid for the supermarket behemoth.

Before the self-service days, most items were not individually packaged and there wasn't much in the way of branding. If you wanted flour, it was just the flour that the shopkeeper had in a large bag. There might have been a couple of options of eggs, for example, but it was the assistant who provided information on the quality so that you could make your decision. With the dawn of self-service, packaging was now the "silent salesperson." This brought with it two fundamental changes: an enormous amount of extra packaging was now needed so that goods could be portioned out and stacked on shelves, and fierce competition grew between brands that were all vying to catch the eye of the customer.

Innovations in packaging materials also transformed the industry. A moisture-proof cellophane was developed and was used in the packaging of a wide range of fresh foods. It sounds obvious to point out, but the key to cellophane's success was the fact that it was *transparent*. Customers could now see what they were buying. Cellophane was also marketed as being more clean and sanitary while promising produce that stayed fresher for longer.

A potato chip manufacturer, called Laura Scudder, is also worth mentioning because she developed the very first potato chip packets. She used wax paper that was ironed into the shape of a bag, filled with chips, and then sealed with glue. Before this, chips were kept in large barrels or glass display cases, which meant they didn't stay fresh for long. Her company was also the first to put freshness dates on its packets.

These two fundamental changes in packaging practices have created challenges for the modern supermarket shopper who wants to make sustainable and ethical choices:

1. Large amounts of (unnecessary and/or environmentally unfriendly) packaging

2. Branding on packaging that often uses aggressive and/or misleading marketing tactics, such as spurious health, environmental, or ethical claims

These challenges (among countless others) would not be such an issue for the conscious customer if it were easier to reject the supermarket model. But it's not so easy. Supermarkets kill off competition from smaller retailers by having plentiful stock at cheap prices—an enticing concept for today's busy and money-conscious families. They have employed the extensive shopping data from loyalty cards to understand consumer habits and behaviors and to successfully expand into insurance, banking, internet, phones, and other areas. Many supermarkets have photo-printing services, pharmacies, and even hairdressers in them. The idea is that customers shouldn't need to go anywhere else. But the truth is that, in many cases, we *can't* go anywhere else. Supermarkets have created a captive market.

We see this in a literal sense when we physically enter the supermarket. Have you ever noticed how difficult it is to leave without buying anything? It's designed this way! And it's not just consumers who are hemmed in by supermarkets. The oligopoly that supermarkets hold in the food retail sector means that small-scale farmers, who produce unbranded goods, have almost no bargaining power. As a result, these farmers often receive a negligible share of the profits while having to bear the risk of unpredictable crops. And it's not just the farmers who are suffering. A 2022 report published by Oxfam on the progress (or lack thereof) of US supermarkets' efforts to address exploitation in their supply chains makes for uncomfortable reading:

> ... the world's frontline food workers remain the most vulnerable to poverty and exploitation, as the largest and most profitable supermarkets continue to exploit them by imposing unrealistic pricing pressure on their suppliers. The food workers that farm, fish, manufacture and sell the food we eat struggle to earn a living wage, access basic health and safety protections, and sometimes even to avoid slave labor conditions. ("Turning Point: A Three-Year Update on US Supermarkets' Progress and Pitfalls." Last modified April 2022.)

So, with such a broken food system so dominantly in place, how can we, as individuals, negotiate our participation in such a system—a system in which most of us have little choice but to participate? Food is, in this sense, a unique case. We cannot simply opt out; everyone needs to eat. Complete self-sufficiency is not a reality for the vast majority. What can we do (or not do)?

I believe that eating seasonally, where possible, is the best place to start. So, let's dive in.

Why Eat Seasonally?

Foods that are in season just taste better. Seasonal produce is fresher; fruits and vegetables are usually picked at their peak ripeness—none of the soft, tasteless apples or tomatoes that feel like bullets. And eating seasonally often means eating locally. It presents an opportunity to support your local farmers while reducing the footprint associated with transportation. It also supports sustainable agricultural practices as it aligns with natural growing seasons and cycles—not fighting against Mother Nature to grow tomatoes in large indoor spaces, with additional heating and light in the middle of winter, or ship them from South America to have a few cherry tomatoes in our salad in mid-January.

Eating seasonally encourages us to diversify our diet as we consume different foods throughout the year depending on what's available. This variety can make meals more exciting and introduce us to new flavors, dishes, and preparation methods. In some areas of the country, it can cost less for both the consumer and the producer, as the supply is high during the peak season, and transportation and storage costs are lower. All of this can bring us closer to where our food comes from.

Seasonal eating also presents an excellent opportunity to experiment with new recipes and cooking techniques. Each season brings its unique flavors, allowing for a diverse range of dishes to play with. Importantly, buying seasonal produce supports local farmers and the local economy. It hopefully also means that your food has traveled shorter distances, reducing its carbon footprint and potential spoilage. These are just a few reasons as to why many environmentalists advocate for local, seasonal eating.

But it's an impossible task to start eating seasonally if we have no idea what's actually in season. Familiarize yourself with what fruits and vegetables are in season during different months in your area. This information can often be found online, in cookbooks, or by asking local farmers and vendors at farmers' markets. One of the best ways to find seasonal produce is to shop at farmers' markets. Here, you can talk directly to growers about their produce and get tips on how to prepare it.

Once you know what's in season, you can start planning your meals accordingly. This might mean trying new recipes or adapting favorite dishes to incorporate seasonal ingredients. This also may look like using roasted butternut squash in your pasta sauce instead of tomatoes or opting for butter bean mash instead of potato. It's hard to imagine what these changes may look like until you make one simple change. With time and practice, it will become easier to pair flavors and adjust according to the seasons.

You might find yourself with more seasonal produce than you can consume at certain times of the year—whether this is from buying a box of discounted tomatoes at your local farm shop or growing too many pickling cucumbers in your own garden. Learning simple preservation methods such as freezing, canning, drying, or pickling can help you enjoy these foods later (see chapter 3 for more on those methods). If you have the space, growing your own fruits and vegetables can be a rewarding way to engage with seasonal eating. Even a small garden or a few pots on a balcony can yield a surprising amount of produce (see chapter 9 for more on gardening).

Be Aware of Greenwashing

Research brands or stores committed to ethical practices and sustainability, and make sure to dig a little deeper. Greenwashing is rife nowadays with brands attaching themselves to any eco-friendly marketing term they can to remain relevant. Good things to look for include fair labor practices, eco-friendly materials, and minimal environmental impact. Websites like Good on You (goodonyou.eco) and *Ethical Consumer* magazine or apps like DoneGood can help you evaluate the ethics and sustainability of different brands. It's best to stay curious and skeptical, and keep asking questions like, Where were your clothes made? Is this just marketing or is it greenwashing? Does the brand provide clear information about their supply chain? What specific practices does a brand implement to minimize their environmental impact? Is there evidence of ongoing efforts to improve their environmental and social impact over time?

Try to find products that come with sustainability certifications, such as fair trade, organic, Rainforest Alliance, or B Corp. These labels indicate adherence to specific ethical and environmental standards, which we'll go through in detail a little later on (see page 19). Certifications have their faults, but they do at least ensure some oversight is happening.

Best Eating Practices by Season

Winter
Focus on hearty root vegetables, squashes, and citrus fruits. These are great for soups, stews, and roasts.

Spring
Enjoy tender leafy greens, asparagus, and strawberries. They're perfect for salads, light pasta dishes, and desserts.

Summer
Take advantage of a variety of berries, stone fruits, and fresh vegetables such as tomatoes and cucumbers for fresh salads, grilling, and refreshing desserts.

Autumn
Embrace apples, pears, pumpkins, and late harvest greens. Ideal for baking, making hearty casseroles, and creating warming soups.

By adopting seasonal eating, you not only enrich your diet with a diversity of fresh and flavorful foods but also contribute to a more sustainable and health-conscious lifestyle—and, therefore, a more conscious kitchen.

Where to Shop Sustainably and Ethically

Okay, so you want to eat more seasonally, perhaps more sustainably, but where do you begin? Let's explore what ethical and sustainable shopping may involve, including accessibility, budget, and transportation.

Stay Local and Consider Secondhand

If in doubt, try to stay local. Shopping locally can reduce your reliance on transportation and directly supports your local economy. Not to mention farmers' markets, local artisans, and small businesses often provide handmade, small-scale, or sustainably produced goods. It's a good rule of thumb to consider the entire life cycle of a product—from production to disposal—because what you see is only half of the story. Products made with recyclable or biodegradable materials are generally more sustainable, but remember that buying secondhand and using what you already have will always be the most sustainable option.

It's no secret that ethical and sustainable shopping can be incredibly expensive, but there are quite a few budget-friendly options to consider. Buying secondhand from thrift stores or online marketplaces, such as Vinted, Depop, and eBay, will always be more sustainable. You're purchasing something already in circulation and preventing it from heading to a landfill. Investing in the occasional quality item could also save you money in the long run, especially if you value and take care of that piece.

Try your best to stay informed about sustainable practices and ethical issues in retail; *Ethical Consumer Magazine* is a great resource for this. Consumer demand for ethical products can drive more businesses to adopt sustainable practices, and conversely boycotting unethical brands is and has been incredibly effective. Remember, every small step toward ethical and sustainable shopping makes a difference. You don't have to do it perfectly; making mindful choices as per your circumstances is a great start.

Ethical Considerations for Certain Foods

In this section, we look into the ethical considerations you should bear in mind while shopping for ingredients. As an example, we'll be looking at three specific products—coffee, vanilla, and sugar—

highlighting the importance of making informed choices that reflect a commitment to sustainability and fair trade practices. It's crucial to recognize that while this section aims to raise awareness and encourage a shift toward more ethical consumption, you must understand that it might not always be feasible to adhere to these guidelines 100 percent of the time. Therefore, I advocate for doing the best you can, acknowledging the effort toward making more responsible choices, even if it's not possible to be perfect. My goal is to offer insights and recommendations that empower you to make decisions that align with your values and the broader implications for communities and the environment.

Coffee

The coffee industry has historically been associated with both child labor and exploitative labor practices, deforestation, and pollution. But we can do many things to ensure that the coffee we're drinking supports sustainable farming practices and farmers. Choosing organic, if we can, is one of them, and buying direct trade coffee is another. This practice involves buying directly from the growers, ensuring more profits go directly to them rather than intermediaries or large corporations.

Today, the coffee industry is one of the world's largest and is often criticized for its continued issues with labor exploitation. However, there has been a growing movement toward ethical sourcing and sustainability, with certifications and consumer awareness playing a pivotal role in driving change.

(Continued on page 23)

Certifications

You should be mindful of a few certifications as you source your food. In the US and UK, certifications are available for food companies, each with their own unique focus and meaning. While certifications aren't perfect, they provide some oversight. Oversight is our greatest asset when trying to combat inequality, and certifications can help us to make more informed decisions. Chances are that if you've been exploring ways to create a conscious kitchen for some time now, your cupboards are no doubt full of products with the certifications below. Included here is a list of the most common certifications. Let's take a look.

Fair Trade

The fair trade certificate represents a standard for ethically produced and traded goods. It focuses on improving trading conditions and promoting sustainable practices.

Ethical standards: It assures consumers that the products meet specific social, environmental, and economic standards. These include fair wages, safe working conditions, and environmentally friendly practices.

Community development: Part of the income from fair trade products is invested back into the community to improve education, health, and infrastructure.

Third-party certification: Fair trade is often certified by independent third parties, enhancing its reliability. Organizations such as Fairtrade International or the Fair Trade Federation are responsible for setting standards and certifying products.

Transparency and accountability: There are rigorous auditing and compliance processes in place to ensure adherence to standards. This includes regular monitoring and reporting.

Certifications such as fair trade look excellent on paper, but it's important to dig a little deeper to understand the actual process a company has to go through to get certified. Here are a few of the hoops brands have to jump through.

First, companies must comply with fair trade standards related to labor, environmental practices, and equitable trading relationships. The company applies for certification and then undergoes an initial audit by a certifying company. Once certified, companies are subject to continuous monitoring and periodic re-auditing to ensure ongoing compliance. Companies also pay a fair trade premium—an additional sum of money on top of the agreed-upon fair trade price—which goes into a communal fund for workers and farmers to use. Finally, companies must demonstrate traceability in their supply chain and be transparent about their business practices.

USDA Organic

This certification is issued by the US Department of Agriculture. It signifies that the food product complies with federal guidelines for organic farming, which include resource cycling, promoting ecological balance, and conserving biodiversity. Products with this label are produced without synthetic fertilizers, pesticides, and other chemicals.

Rainforest Alliance Certified

This certification emphasizes sustainable farming practices that protect rainforests and the wildlife within them. It also focuses on fair treatment and good working conditions for workers.

Marine Stewardship Council (MSC)

This is an international certification focusing on sustainable fishing practices. Products with the MSC label indicate that the seafood comes from a fishery that has been independently assessed on its impacts on wild fish populations and the ecosystems where it operates.

Leaping Bunny

Although not directly related to food, the Leaping Bunny certification is common in the UK and US for cruelty-free products, including in some food and beverage categories. It ensures that no new animal testing has been used in any phase of product development.

B Corporation Certification

This certification is for businesses as a whole rather than individual products. B Corps are companies that meet high standards of social and environmental performance, transparency, and accountability.

Non-GMO Project Verified

This label signifies that a product has been independently verified to be free of genetically modified organisms. It's a common certification in the US for food products.

Red Tractor

Predominantly seen in the UK, this certification assures that food products are traceable, safe to eat, and have been produced responsibly. It covers a range of standards, including food safety, animal welfare, and environmental protection.

Soil Association

This is a UK-based certification for organic food and farming. Products with this label meet high environmental and animal welfare standards.

Fair trade certification is arguably the most reliable indication of ethical and sustainable practices regarding the production and trade of goods. It requires companies to adhere to strict standards and undergo rigorous monitoring, thus offering consumers what seems like a trustworthy choice for socially and environmentally responsible products. Since the companies must undergo periodic re-auditing, it's best to keep an eye on your favorite brands to ensure they're still receiving the certificate.

Each certification has its own set of standards and requirements, and companies typically undergo rigorous assessments and audits to obtain and maintain these certifications. They are designed to give consumers confidence about the quality and sustainability of the products they purchase.

WE FOUNDED Hᵤ TO UNITE
ULTRASIMPLE™ INGREDIENTS
WITH UNBEATABLE TASTE.

L3345B   16:29
BBD   06/11/25

ORGANIC
FAIRTRADE
48% COCOA

NO REFINED SUGAR
NO CANE SUGAR
NO SUGAR ALCOHOLS
NO ERYTHRITOL
NO SOY/GLUTEN
NO PALM OIL
NO LECITHINS
NO EMULSIFIERS

USDA
ORGANIC

FAIRTRADE

K D

CUR-D-187

Nutrition Facts

2 servings per container

Serving size **1/2 bar (30g)**

Amount per serving	
Calories	**180**

	% Daily Value*
Total Fat 13g	17%
Saturated Fat 8g	40%
Cholesterol 5mg	2%
Sodium 35mg	2%
Total Carbohydrate 13g	5%
Dietary Fiber 2g	7%
Total Sugars 10g	14%
Includes 7g Added Sugars	8%
Protein 3g	6%
Calcium 98mg	6%
Iron 3mg	15%
Potassium 249mg	5%

Not a significant source of trans fat and
vitamin D

*The % Daily Value (DV) tells you how much a nutrient in a
serving of food contributes to a daily diet. 2,000 calories a
day is used for general nutrition advice.

@HUKITCHEN

GET BACK TO HUM...

Here are a few certifications you can look for when considering different coffee brands:

Fair Trade Certified: Ensures fair prices, workers' rights, community development, and environmental sustainability.

Organic Certified: Guarantees the coffee is grown without synthetic fertilizers or chemicals.

Rainforest Alliance Certified: Focuses on environmentally sustainable and socially responsible agriculture practices.

UTZ Certified: Ensures sustainable farming and better opportunities for farmers, their families, and our planet.

Bird-Friendly Certification: The Smithsonian Migratory Bird Center ensures coffee is shade-grown and organic, preserving bird habitats.

Sugar

The history of sugar is as long as it is bleak, and unfortunately human rights breaches and environmental degradation remain fundamental issues within the industry. Buying from ethical sugar brands and opting for organic and fair trade sugar can help mitigate these issues somewhat, but it's important to remember that these issues still exist and we should be mindful of their impact. When buying sugar, I look for both the fair trade certification as well as the organic certification.

Vanilla

Vanilla is a fascinating plant, and its story is just as interesting. I came across the vanilla orchid in Denver's botanical garden a few years ago, and it piqued my interest in the history of our food. The vanilla orchid needs to be hand-pollinated, a discovery made in 1841 by an enslaved boy named Edmond

Albius on the island of Réunion. This method, which is still used today, is incredibly labor intensive. Once grown, the beans then undergo a time-consuming sun-drying process and sweating (a process where the beans are wrapped in cloth and cycle between hot and cool environments), taking about one year to go from implantation to export.

Vanilla is one of the most expensive spices, second only to saffron, due to the labor and skill required for its cultivation and processing. In fact, most of the vanilla flavor in products is actually artificial. The economic instability and challenges in vanilla cultivation, including theft and premature harvesting, have led to the reliance on artificial vanilla flavoring derived from different by-products.

Due to vanilla's high price, it is challenging for people on a budget to support smaller farms by purchasing the whole bean. So do your best to avoid vanilla, buy the whole bean, or buy other products with certifications.

How to Shop in Bulk

Now that you've read up on ethical considerations when shopping, let's discuss the actual practice of shopping itself and how to navigate bulk and zero-waste shops. Bulk shopping refers to the practice of purchasing items in large quantities or in larger-than-average sizes. This approach is commonly adopted for a variety of reasons. Buying in bulk often results in a lower cost per unit, making it a cost-effective option for many items, most notably things such as rice, beans, and pasta. It can potentially also reduce the amount of packaging waste, as the items are often packaged in larger containers or even available without individual packaging. A big draw to purchasing in bulk is the amount of time saved by reducing the frequency of shopping trips, and it allows con-

Why Are Zero-Waste Stores Expensive?

Zero-waste shops often have higher prices due to the quality of their food and the sourcing of products, as well as their eco-friendly packaging and economies of scale. Zero-waste shops typically prioritize high-quality, sustainable, and often organic products. These items are generally more expensive to produce due to higher production standards, ethical sourcing, and sometimes smaller scale production. The cost of sustainable packaging materials can be higher than conventional packaging as well. These shops avoid plastic and other nonrecyclable materials, opting for biodegradable or reusable alternatives, which are more costly.

Many zero-waste shops are small businesses and don't benefit from the economies of scale that larger retailers do. Big stores reduce cost through bulk purchasing and mass production, a benefit smaller shops can't match. Sourcing products from ethical and sustainable suppliers often involves a more complex and expensive supply chain, with higher costs for transportation, especially if the products are sourced from local or small-scale producers. Zero-waste products also have a much smaller market than its big store competition. The lower demand can lead to higher per-unit costs, as fixed costs (such as rent, utilities, and labor) are distributed over a smaller volume of sales.

I've had some very honest conversations with owners of zero-waste shops, and there's no doubt that they do it to help create a better, less wasteful world and make zero-waste shopping more accessible. While prices need to come down to make zero-waste shopping more accessible for more shoppers, we also need viable solutions to support shop owners. If only zero-waste shops were subsidized, rather than big corporations, that dream might become a reality.

sumers to maintain a well-stocked pantry or supply of ingredients, which can be particularly useful for items that are used frequently.

However, bulk shopping also has its drawbacks. It requires significant storage space and might lead to waste if the items are perishable and not used before their expiration date. It's also important for shoppers to consider whether they will realistically use large quantities of the items, to avoid unnecessary purchases. Another consideration is price.

Of course, you are getting a larger quantity of the ingredients you're after, but that will mean shelling out more money at once. Many people simply cannot do this and are unable to take advantage of the potential savings.

Bulk Shopping at a Zero-Waste Store

Zero-waste stores are exactly what food shopping should look like. Tall shelves with towering jars full of healthy whole foods that can be purchased in any amount. There are often large barrels full of oats with shiny metal scoops waiting to be used. Bulk shopping at a zero-waste store is a completely different experience than at a supermarket. Their approach is to do the hard work for you, and to make shopping ethically and sustainably as easy as possible. The trouble is that these stores are expensive for both the owner and the consumer. Here's how it works:

Shoppers are encouraged or required to bring their own reusable containers. These can be glass jars, cloth bags, or other suitable containers that are clean and ready to use. Before filling jars or bags, containers are usually weighed (or "tared") to ensure that the weight of the container is not included in the price of the product. Stores usually offer a variety of products in bulk bins or dispensers. Shoppers can fill their containers with the exact amount they need, which helps to reduce food waste and allows for the purchase of smaller quantities, if desired. After filling containers, they are weighed again, and the price is calculated based on the weight of the product.

Products I've found to be commonly available at zero-waste stores include:

Dry goods: Grains, nuts, cereals, pasta, and legumes

Spices and herbs: A variety of spices and dried herbs

Liquids: Oils, vinegars, syrups, and liquid soaps and cleaning products

Personal care items: Bar soaps, shampoos, conditioners, and lotions, often available in refillable formats

Although zero-waste stores have faced some criticism, there are many benefits to supporting them. Since products are not prepackaged, zero-waste shopping significantly reduces the amount of plastic and other packaging materials consumed. You can buy exactly the amount you need, which is particularly useful for spices, herbs, or other products used in small quantities. Zero-waste stores often source products from ethical and sustainable producers, doing most of the hard work for us before we even step in the door. These stores often serve as a hub for learning about sustainability and waste reduction—which I can attest to, having spent many a night getting advice from my local shop owners.

However, it's important to note that accessibility to zero-waste stores can be a challenge in some areas, and the cost of products may sometimes be higher compared with those at conventional retail stores. Despite these challenges, zero-waste bulk shopping is growing in popularity as a means of reducing our personal environmental impact.

In this chapter, we've explored the essentials of ethical and sustainable shopping, highlighting the significance of recognizing certifications, the benefits of bulk buying, the ethos behind zero-waste stores, and the ethical nuances of commodities such as coffee, vanilla, and sugar. Ethical shopping isn't just a transaction; it's a statement of our values and a step toward a more sustainable future. Yes, zero-waste stores might come with a price premium and finding ethically sourced goods can require a bit more effort, but the impact of these choices extends far beyond our immediate convenience. By thoughtfully choosing where and how we shop, we contribute to a global movement toward sustainability, supporting practices that respect both people and the planet. I hope, however, that this chapter serves as a guide and an inspiration for making shopping choices that align with a more conscious and ethical world.

2

STORING FOOD

In this chapter, we'll look at some of the practices for storing food effectively, reducing food waste and minimizing plastic in our kitchens. These strategies benefit not only the environment but also our health and budget. We'll begin by exploring the various food storage methods, focusing on techniques that extend the shelf life of perishables and maintain the quality of dried goods. Understanding the correct storage methods for different types of food is crucial in preventing premature spoilage and waste.

Next, we'll address pantry staples and kitchen essentials. This section offers practical tips on planning meals from cupboard essentials and creating a system so that you remember what you have available. We'll learn how to make the most out of our groceries and how small changes in our daily habits can significantly reduce the amount of food we throw away.

Finally, we'll look at the history of sell-by dates, how accurate they are, and why we should often ignore them. By the end of this chapter, you will be equipped with the knowledge and skills to make your conscious kitchen organized and sustainable.

What's the Problem with Food Waste?

Food waste is usually edible items thrown away, often unnecessarily, due to overbuying, improper storage, or confusing food labels. Food waste occurs at various supply chain stages, from production and processing to retail and consumption.

As agricultural and food production technologies have advanced, the sheer volume of food produced has increased dramatically. However, this increase in quantity often comes with inefficiencies in the supply chain. Large amounts of food are lost or wasted due to spoilage, logistical challenges, or cosmetic standards set by retailers that reject perfectly edible food for not meeting specific aesthetic criteria. These high standards often hurt farmers the most and necessitate the need for food rescue companies, such as Oddbox and Imperfect Foods, and nonprofits.

In many developed countries, consumer habits contribute significantly to food waste. The abundance of food and relatively low prices lead to over-purchasing. Additionally, busy lifestyles result in more eating out, leading to the neglect of the food we have at home. There is also a need for more awareness about keeping different types of food properly, which we will cover in this chapter. Furthermore, there is often confusion over "best before," "sell by," and "use by" dates, meaning that consumers will throw food away that is perfectly edible due to a general misconception that food is not safe to consume past these dates, but this simply isn't true.

Food waste is not just an economic issue but also a primary environmental concern. When food is wasted, all the resources used for growing, processing, packing, transporting, and marketing it are wasted too—this includes water, land, labor, and capital. Moreover, when food waste ends up in landfills, it decomposes anaerobically, producing methane, a potent greenhouse gas contributing to climate change.

The irony of food waste becomes particularly stark when considering global hunger issues. Millions of people around the world suffer from food insecurity and malnutrition, making the massive amounts of wasted food a stark reminder of global inequality. The economic implications of food waste are also significant. It represents a substantial loss of economic value for farmers, retailers, and consumers. Food wasted literally means money down the drain.

In response to these challenges, numerous initiatives and strategies are being adopted globally. These range from governmental policies and corporate responsibility programs to grassroots campaigns focused on educating consumers about food preservation and responsible purchasing. Reducing food waste is seen not just as an environmental or economic necessity but as a moral imperative in a world grappling with issues of sustainability and equitable resource distribution.

How to Shop to Reduce Waste

So how may we shop to reduce waste? We can use many tools to keep costs down and waste lower. Take what is applicable for you now and maybe in the future, and simply leave the rest. Small, incremental changes make the most difference because they compound over time and require more subtle habit change. Any book you read on behavior change (such as *Tiny Habits* by BJ Fogg or *Atomic Habits* by James Clear) will tell you to start small, tiny, or "atomic." Tiny requires little motivation, a small amount of schedule change, and, yet, a huge amount of growth. Here are some of the tools I use daily, weekly, or monthly to reduce waste while shopping:

1. Before shopping, plan your meals for the week. This helps in buying only what you need, thereby reducing the chances of purchasing excess food that might go to waste.

2. Create a detailed shopping list based on your meal plan. Avoid impulse buys that might not fit into your meal plans and could lead to waste.

3. Learn the difference between "best before" and "use by" dates to avoid discarding food that is still safe to eat. We'll cover this on page 35.

4. Purchase fruits and vegetables in amounts you can realistically consume before they spoil, or create a plan for freezing, drying, or preserving the excess in other ways.

5. Supermarkets will discount fruits and vegetables that are perfectly edible but visually imperfect. These are often wasted, so buying them helps reduce waste and is kinder on your wallet.

6. Only buy in bulk if you're sure you can consume the items before they expire. Bulk buying is great for nonperishables, such as rice or pasta, and of course helps to reduce plastic waste if you're able to bring your own containers.

7. Purchase exactly the amount you need from bulk bins to avoid excess and reduce packaging waste, if available to you.

8. If you accidentally buy too much, freeze what you can for later use.

9. Use supermarkets and stores that have policies to donate unsold food to shelters or food banks.

10. Join a CSA.

11. Buy loose leaf tea or whole coffee beans. It reduces packaging waste, and you can buy the exact amount you need.

12. When planning meals, use perishable items first to ensure they don't go bad.

13. Proper storage can significantly extend the life of food products. Learn the best ways to store different types of food in the following pages.

14. For foods you don't use often, consider buying them preserved or canned to extend their shelf life.

15. If you can afford to do so, shop at farmers' markets, which often offer fresh produce that hasn't undergone long transportation and storage periods, reducing the chances of premature spoiling.

16. Grow what you can, with what you have. A pot of herbs here or a jar of sprouts there can contribute to the overall sustainability of your home.

There are so many more ways to shop sustainably, including some excellent tips from behavior change experts, such as never shop hungry and only in the mornings, but these basics will start you off on the right foot as you set out to create your conscious kitchen. I want to give you the tools to find what works for you, while also empowering you to experiment on your own.

How to Store Fresh Produce to Reduce Waste

Food storage is a surprisingly undervalued tool for reducing waste. Depending on the type of produce, what it's wrapped in, and where it's placed, a piece of fruit can last between five days and two weeks. Below I have outlined some ideal ways to store specific foods. Each type of produce has its own best method of storage to maintain freshness and flavor, and these methods can help you get the most out of your fruits and vegetables.

Produce	Storage Method
Apples	Store in a cool, dark place. If refrigerated, keep in a crisper drawer away from vegetables.
Asparagus	Store upright in a glass of water in the refrigerator, like a bouquet of flowers.
Avocados	Store at room temperature until ripe, then refrigerate if not using immediately.
Berries	Store in the refrigerator in their original container or a covered bowl. Do not wash until ready to eat.
Carrots	Refrigerate in a plastic bag with holes or in the crisper drawer. Keep them away from fruits that emit ethylene gas. If they become a little soft, place them in a bowl of water in the fridge for a few hours.
Celery	Store in the refrigerator to maintain freshness and crispness.
Citrus Fruits (Oranges, Lemons, Limes)	Store in a cool place, in either a fruit bowl or the refrigerator.
Cucumbers	Store in the refrigerator crisper drawer, wrapped in a tea towel and placed in a stasher bag.
Garlic	Store in a cool, dry place with good air circulation.
Herbs (Basil, Cilantro, Parsley)	Store like asparagus (in a glass of water) or wrap in a damp tea towel and place in a stasher bag in the refrigerator.
Leafy Greens (Lettuce, Spinach, Kale)	Wrap in a damp tea towel and store in the refrigerator in a container or plastic bag if any need reusing.
Mushrooms	Store in the refrigerator in their original packaging or a paper bag. Avoid plastic bags, which can cause moisture buildup.
Onions	Store in a cool, dry, well-ventilated area. Keep away from potatoes.

Peaches, Plums, Nectarines	Store at room temperature until ripe, then refrigerate to extend freshness.
Peppers (Bell, Chili)	Store in the refrigerator crisper drawer. If you have one to reuse, keep in a plastic bag for extended freshness.
Potatoes	Store in a cool, dark, and well-ventilated place. Avoid storing with onions, as they emit gases that can accelerate spoilage.
Tomatoes	Store at room temperature away from sunlight. Refrigerate only when fully ripe to extend life.
Sweet Corn	Keep in the refrigerator with husks on to retain moisture.
Zucchini and Summer Squash	Store in the refrigerator crisper drawer.

How to Store Pantry Items to Reduce Waste

This section works as a guide on how to store your pantry staples effectively and includes an example chart of the different kinds of ingredients you may find useful to stock. The chart is organized into grains, nuts and seeds, pulses, and baking. A well-organized pantry is the backbone of any kitchen, enabling you to keep ingredients fresh, reduce food waste, and make meal preparation simpler and more enjoyable. Here you will find practical advice and tips for storing various pantry items, understanding date labels, and kitchen tools you may find helpful.

These items are great for long-term storage and can be used in a variety of dishes to make vegan and vegetarian cooking both nutritious and tasty. Storing grains, seeds, and pulses correctly is crucial for maintaining their quality and extending their shelf life.

Grains	Nuts and Seeds	Pulses	Baking
Barley	Cashews	Black beans	All-purpose flour
Cornmeal	Chia seeds	Black-eyed peas	Baking powder
Couscous	Flaxseeds	Butter beans	Baking soda
Oats (rolled oats, steel-cut oats)	Hemp seeds	Chickpeas	Bread flour
Pasta (various types such as spaghetti, penne)	Peanuts	Kidney beans	Caster sugar
	Pecans	Lentils (red, green, brown, black)	Flaky sea salt
Quinoa	Poppy seeds	Navy beans	Semolina
Rice (basmati, brown, jasmine)	Pumpkin seeds (pepitas)	Pinto beans	Soft brown sugar
	Sunflower seeds	Split peas (green and yellow)	Whole-wheat flour

Let's take a look at some of the best ways to store dried goods in your conscious kitchen.

Airtight Containers

Use glass or metal containers with airtight seals for grains, seeds, and pulses. Airtight containers prevent exposure to air, moisture, and pests, which can spoil these items. They also help maintain the flavor and texture of the ingredients. Using reusable containers reduces plastic waste and is more sustainable than disposable packaging.

Cool, Dark, and Dry Storage

Store your containers in a cool, dark, and dry place, such as a pantry or cupboard. Exposure to light and heat can degrade the quality of grains, seeds, and pulses, leading to quicker spoilage. A dry environment prevents mold growth and insect infestations.

Vacuum Sealing

For long-term storage, consider vacuum sealing grains and pulses. This method removes air from the package, extending shelf life significantly. Vacuum-sealed bags are reusable and reduce the need for frequent purchasing, thus reducing food waste.

Should We Be Concerned with Plastic?

Plastic pollution poses a significant threat to our planet, and our kitchens are often major contributors to this problem. There are a number of ways to reduce plastic usage, from choosing alternative materials to adopting zero-waste practices. However, like with all suggestions in this book, you should adopt what you can and what works for your lifestyle. The conscious kitchen should be, first and foremost, accessible.

Tips for Reducing Plastic

Reducing plastic in your kitchen involves a combination of avoiding single-use plastics, opting for sustainable materials, and, honestly, just doing your best.

Once your plastic containers begin to wear out, consider replacing them with glass or stainless-steel options. These materials last longer and are safer for storing food. Secondhand shops seem to be teeming with reusable glass jars you can use, or simply reusing the jars that things such as pasta sauce and pickles come in is a free and sustainable alternative. Opt for utensils and kitchen tools made of wood or metal instead of plastic. These are more durable and environmentally friendly. Use soy wax wraps, cloth covers, or silicone lids instead of plastic wrap and aluminum foil for covering and storing food. Purchase food in bulk to reduce packaging waste. Bring your own containers or bags to the store to avoid using plastic packaging. Choose products that come in paper, glass, or metal packaging instead of plastic. This can apply to everything from food products to cleaning supplies. Always carry reusable shopping bags to avoid plastic bags.

Properly recycle any unavoidable plastic and find creative ways to upcycle items, although there is no need to hold on to plastic items that you simply cannot use. If recycling options are limited, I encourage you to use the letter template on page 172 to ask your local representatives to change this. (The template is for composting, but it can be easily adjusted for recycling.) Make your own cleaning products using natural ingredients and store them in reusable containers to avoid plastic packaging. Or support independent brands providing plastic-free tabs that are designed to be dissolved. Rather than using plastic bin bags, compost your organic kitchen waste. Check out chapter 9 to learn more. And if you're feeling particularly community driven, share your practices with friends and family to create a larger impact.

Freezing

Some seeds and grains can be stored in the freezer to extend their shelf life. Freezing is especially useful for seeds high in oils (such as flaxseeds) that can go rancid quickly at room temperature. Ensure they are in airtight, moisture-proof containers or bags to prevent freezer burn.

Labeling and Rotation

Clearly label each container with the contents and the date of purchase or packaging. Use a "first-in, first-out" system, where older items are used before newer ones. This practice ensures that ingredients are used before they expire or lose quality.

How to Understand Date Labels

The terms "best before," "sell by," and "use by" are all date labels used on food packaging, but they serve different purposes:

Best before date: This indicates the date up to which the food product will maintain its optimal quality and flavor. The product should still be safe to consume after this date, but it might not be at its best in terms of taste or texture.

Sell by date: This is used by retailers as a guide for inventory management. It tells the store how long to display the product for sale. Consumers can still use the product after the "sell by" date, as it is not a safety date.

Use by date: This is the last date recommended for the use of the product while at peak quality. In some cases, especially with perishable items, the "use by" date is also a health safety indicator, implying that the product should not be consumed after this date.

The concept of these dates began to gain prominence in the twentieth century, particularly as consumer awareness about food safety grew. The exact origin of these terms is a bit murky, but they became more standardized and widespread with the advent of consumer protection laws and food safety regulations in the latter half of the twentieth century.

Their relevance today is a subject of debate. While they are meant to guide consumers about food quality and safety, they can also contribute to food waste. Many people discard food items after the "best before" or "sell by" dates, not realizing that these products are often still safe and consumable. To address this, there have been efforts in various countries to standardize these labels for better clarity and to reduce unnecessary waste. The use of these dates is still considered relevant for food safety and quality, but there is a growing emphasis on educating consumers about what these dates really mean.

Understanding these dates, as well as implementing the storage tips listed earlier in this chapter, will ensure that your food lasts as long as possible and will cut down on your overall food waste. Food preservation goes hand in hand with food storage and perfectly complements these methods to keep fresh food usable for longer. We'll cover that in detail in the next chapter.

FERMENTATION AND OTHER FOOD PRESERVATIONS

In this chapter we'll explore the methods, techniques, and recipes that have made both preservation and fermentation enduring practices across the world. Moreover, we will discover how these ancient preservation methods not only elevate the taste and texture of foods but also extend their shelf life, allowing us to savor the seasons and reduce waste. In a conscious kitchen, food preservation serves as a vital technique to extend the longevity of our food, ensuring that the produce from one season can be enjoyed throughout the year. This practice not only reduces food waste but also enhances our connection to local food systems and seasonal eating. By preserving food, we honor the energy and resources that have gone into its production, making the most of every harvest and supporting sustainability in our daily lives.

From the transformative magic of fermentation, which gives us foods such as sauerkraut, kimchi, and sourdough, to the time-honored practices of canning, drying, and pickling, each method offers unique benefits and flavors. They allow us to preserve not just food but our hard work too. So, whether you're fairly confident in the kitchen or a complete beginner, this chapter aims to inspire and empower you to give the magic of fermentation a go and explore preservation in your own home.

The Magic of Fermentation

I'll never forget my introduction into the world of fermentation. It was a tangy explosion of flavor contained in a small glass jar that my mum had bought from an alternative health food shop. At first, I was skeptical. I couldn't understand how a simple ingredient had been transformed into this sour, yet delicious food. So, like any other curious individual, I spent hours researching "how to make weird-smelling cabbage that tastes good" and discovered the world of sauerkraut. I thought to myself, *How hard can this be? It's just cabbage and salt.* And just like that, I started my journey learning everything I could about preserving food.

As I dove deep into fermentation, I learned how to make food last longer or change the flavor, how to make something fizzy, and how fermentation can alter the texture of our food.

Simple ferments such as hot sauce, pickles, and sauerkraut were just the beginning. I started to think about wild ingredients and the role of foraging. Every spring I walked through the fields behind my parents' house in search of wild garlic. The long, fragrant leaves can be used to make pesto or a rich salt or can be added to sauerkraut to diversify its flavor profile. Next, I began to look at nettles, a fierce enemy of every child who spent their summers running through tall grass. Nettles have recently been heralded as a wonder weed that can feed your plants, produce a nutrient-rich tea, and even form seeds that offer a natural energy boost. The more I learned, the more I realized just how exciting even the most innocuous plant can be.

Every walk or hike became a practice in simply noticing. How far along are the pears on our neighbor's tree, whose branches hang heavy with the ripening fruit? Are the blackberries sweet enough to pick to make the first apple crumble of the season? And have the mushrooms returned to that favorite spot that boasted enormous flushes the year before? Fruits, vegetables, and herbs no longer just exist. They sit in the tiny compartment of my mind that constantly wonders: *What would this batch of kombucha taste like if I added wild elderberries? And how can I make it even fizzier?*

This is the magic of fermentation. A world of wonder and mystery waiting to be explored.

According to Sandor Katz in *The Art of Fermentation* (Chelsea, VT: Chelsea Green Publishing, 2012), fermentation is "the transformative action of microorganisms." Fermentation is a natural metabolic process driven by microorganisms such as bacteria, yeasts, and molds that convert sugars and other organic compounds into different compounds, often involving the production of alcohol, acids, or gases. When it comes to food, fermentation is used to enhance flavors and extend shelf life and is often claimed to increase nutritional value. This process can be found in some of our favorite foods, such as yogurt, sourdough, wine, beer, and soy sauce. Fermentation gives yogurt its sourness, beer its alcohol content, and soy sauce its deep umami flavor. So, as you can see, the art of fermentation is truly remarkable and can be an invaluable resource for those wanting to expand their skills and experience in the kitchen.

Types of Fermentation

Before we can get started with the practical aspects of fermentation, let's take a look at the different categories that fermentations fall into. Lactic acid bacteria are some of the most common microbes found in today's fermented foods, such as kimchi, sauerkraut, and cheese. The acidic environment that these microbes create prevents more harmful microbes from overtaking and potentially spoiling the food. Tempeh, for example, utilizes *Rhizopus oligosporus*, which thrives at higher temperatures and overgrows the soybeans in around eighteen hours. The acidic conditions, lack of water, and high temperatures all contribute to the safety of producing tempeh at home. A few things that differentiate ferments from one another are the kind of bacteria present, the percentage of salt used, and of course the foundational ingredient.

According to microbiologist Keith H. Steinkraus in his 1997 paper on the classification of fermented foods, home-fermented foods fall into seven basic categories:

1. Textured vegetable proteins: These are made from legumes or cereals and will include things such as tempeh from Indonesia.

2. Lactic acid fermentations: This includes lacto-fermented vegetables and grains, such as sauerkraut, kimchi, pickles, and so on.

3. Yeast-leavened breads: This is where we find things such as sourdough and store-bought yeast, often called dried active yeast.

4. Amino sauces and pastes: Familiar things such as miso, shoyu, and soy sauce fall into this category.

5. Alkaline ferments: Japanese natto is perhaps the most widely recognized example of alkaline ferments, though they are also commonly used in African cuisines, such as Nigerian ogiri and dawadawa, Sierra Leone ogiri-saro, and West African iru.

6. Alcohol fermentations: Wine, beer, mead, sake, and so on are all examples of alcohol fermentations. These are generally yeast fermentations, but they can also include yeastlike molds. This process is generally anaerobic to prevent the ethanol content from being oxidized to acetic acid.

7. Acetic acid fermentations: These include things we all most likely have in our cupboards, such as vinegars.

The recipes we'll predominantly look at utilize lactic acid, acetic acid, and yeast-leavened breads. As you can see, from a quick look at the categories, these methods have been used throughout history and across many cultures, producing the foundations for many cultural dishes. There is much debate around what the first ferment actually was, but what we can draw from the information available to us is that fermentation not only shaped the way we eat today but also shaped our bodies and their ability to consume substances such as alcohol.

Tools to Get Started

The most basic tools you'll need are mason jars with lids, a sharp knife, and a weighing scale. If you're looking to upgrade a few items you already have or want some fermentation-specific tools, I recommend fermentation lids that have a gauge on top that allow the bubbles to release without having to do so manually. Weights are also a good tool to use as they're often made with mason jars in mind, so they fit perfectly. Weights help to keep your ingredients submerged in the brine and prevent the ferment from spoiling.

For temperature control, I use a bread proofing box as this allows me flexibility to proof bread, create tempeh, ferment hot sauces, and keep my sourdough starter bubbling away. This isn't necessary and is definitely for those who are avid fermenters and bread makers. If you have a cold house, simply place your ferments in the warmest spot you have. They will likely just need a little more time to develop.

Rules to Abide by on Your Home-Fermented Journey

Some of the best beginner-friendly ferments are the ones that require few ingredients and materials you most likely already have. Sauerkraut is among the easiest, so this is where we'll start. When we purchase fermented foods in the store, we often are paying for the labor rather than the ingredients, and rightly so. Ferments take time, need care and attention, and require specific conditions in which to thrive. Tempeh is a great example of this. When it comes to fermenting foods, I like to abide by a few rules:

1. **Always sterilize your containers before using them for fermentation.** If your containers are in bad condition or not properly cleaned, they can allow bad bacteria to get into your ferments and ruin all your hard work. You can put them through the dishwasher, or if you don't have a dishwasher, boil some water and then pour boiling water over the jars, tools, and lids. We want to have everything as clean as possible before starting. Then wash the items with dish soap and pour boiling water over them again. Place them in the oven at 230°F (110°C) for 10 to 15 minutes until dry, then remove and allow to cool. You can also use a water canner to sterilize your jars, if you have one.

2. **If you're using mason jars,** these can be reused almost indefinitely, but you'll most likely need to replace the lids if you don't take care of them, as they're very prone to rusting. Mason jar lids are cheap and available in most grocery, hardware, and all-purpose stores.

3. **If you're buying new mason jars,** make sure they are good quality and suitable for fermentation. They need to be able to withstand the fermentation process, which creates a lot of pressure within the container.

4. **If fermenting on a larger scale,** you can also use ceramic fermentation pots, which allow the air to escape and utilize water to prevent the introduction of air. Plastic food-grade tubs can also be used, and you can even buy specialized kimchi fermentation tubs from places such as H Mart.

Bubbling Over: Delicious Fermented Recipes

Now that we've addressed the fundamentals of what fermentation actually is, and what you will need, here are a few simple recipes to get you started.

Signs Your Ferment Has Gone Wrong

If your ferment smells rotten or has fuzzy mold growing on the surface, the vegetables have become overly slimy, or your ferment has a rancid taste, throw it out! We all hate to waste food, especially when we've put a lot of hard work and time into a project, but it's important to stay safe when experimenting in the kitchen.

If your ferment grew mold, this could be because the vegetables or other ingredients were not fully submerged in the brine. The brine is an incredibly important liquid that essentially seals off the ferment from oxygen, creating an environment where mold cannot grow.

SIMPLE SAUERKRAUT

1 green cabbage,
sliced thin

Salt

/

Yield: 1-quart (1 L) jar

If this is your first try, use 1 green cabbage and 2 percent salt. This is all you need for a simple beginner-friendly sauerkraut.

First you need to work out how much salt you'll need. Weigh your cabbage (make sure to account for the weight of the vessel) on a food scale. Once you have this measurement, calculate what 2 percent of the weight of the cabbage is; that's how much salt you need. For example, if your cabbage weighs 2,000 g (71 ounces), your salt will be 40 g (1 ounce). I find it easiest to calculate it like this: weight of cabbage × 0.02 = weight of salt.

Place the cabbage in a large mixing bowl and sprinkle the salt over the top. Massage the salt into the cabbage until all the liquid has been released, approximately 5 to 10 minutes. This liquid forms your brine, which will prevent the cabbage from growing mold. Transfer the cabbage to a sterilized jar and cover with the brine, making sure to leave 2 inches (5 cm) of space above the brine to allow gas bubbles to release. Use a sterilized weight to keep the cabbage submerged, or fold one of the outer cabbage leaves and place on top of the content of the jar. You can then use the cabbage core to keep the content submerged. Now loosely screw your lid onto the jar and place it in a corner out of direct sunlight.

Depending on the time of year, your sauerkraut could take 2 to 3 weeks to ferment fully. I usually wait until the bubbles have subsided and then give it a taste. If I like where it's at, I'll move it to the fridge. If not, I'll give it another week.

STORING
You can store your sauerkraut in the fridge while you eat it. It will continue to very slowly ferment, so be sure to finish it before it goes beyond your taste.

I'm a fan of the fermentation lids available, as they have a gauge on top that allows the bubbles to release, but they're not necessary.

Sauerkraut Variations

The beauty of sauerkraut is its ability to be altered to suit your taste. In the spring, I recommend adding wild garlic, chives, or dill and in the fall, adding thinly sliced carrots. Simple additions can really elevate your sauerkraut. When creating variations, which I encourage you to do, make sure that you weigh the entirety of your ingredients so you can always work in percentages. For example, for the beet sauerkraut, weigh the cabbage, beets, and orange zest and take the overall weight and multiply by 0.02 to get your salt ratio.

DILL SAUERKRAUT	SAUERKRAUT WITH CARROT AND FENNEL SEED	RED SAUERKRAUT WITH BEETS AND ORANGE ZEST AND FENNEL SEED
1 green cabbage, sliced thin	1 green cabbage, sliced thin	1 red cabbage, sliced thin
1 bunch fresh dill	1 tablespoon (5.8 g) fennel seeds	1 teaspoon orange zest
Salt	2 medium-size carrots, grated	2 medium-size beets, grated
/	Salt	Salt
Yield: 1-quart (1 L) jar	/	/
	Yield: 1-quart (1 L) jar	Yield: 1-quart (1 L) jar

A Note on Tempeh

If you've watched any of my cooking videos, you'll know that I've become fascinated by tempeh and its variations. But what even is tempeh? Well, tempeh is a white mold-covered cake traditionally made from soybeans whose interaction with fungus neatly knits together the beans to form a solid block, also known as a cake. Tempeh originated from Indonesia, Java to be specific, but soon spread to the rest of Indonesia and Malaysia. The name *tempeh* became more broadly used to refer to any fermented legume or cereal that mycelium had penetrated and bound together.

I was first introduced to tempeh in London when it seemed to soar in popularity among the vegan community as a way to get in another source of plant-based protein. Suddenly, large supermarkets were carrying one or two different brands of tempeh, and it became a normal part of many vegan and vegetarian food shops. The store-bought tempeh was often a little bitter, dull in color, and very bland. So, I wasn't convinced. That all changed, though, when I tasted fresh tempeh, which has a much lighter, nuttier taste with no bitterness whatsoever—but is surprisingly hard to find. This is when I decided to try making it at home, which seemed intimidating at first, but the benefit far outweighs the effort.

If you're interested in making your own tempeh at home, I highly recommend the book *Miso, Tempeh, Natto & Other Tasty Ferments* by Kirsten K. Shockey and Christopher Shockey. This book taught me everything I know.

SCOTCH BONNET AND SWEET PEPPER HOT SAUCE

12 Scotch bonnet
peppers, seeds removed,
chopped into 1-inch
(3 cm) pieces

2 medium-size sweet
peppers, chopped into
1-inch (3 cm) pieces

Half of a yellow onion,
roughly chopped

6 garlic cloves

2–4% salt

AFTER FERMENTATION

3 tablespoons (44 ml)
apple cider vinegar

½ cup (118 ml) brine

/

Yield: 12-ounce
(355 ml) jar

Hot sauce is a great beginner-friendly ferment because it's simple, easy to adapt, and mostly requires patience.

You will need a mason jar with a lid, a weight, and weighing scales.

Add the hot peppers, sweet peppers, onion, and garlic to a sterilized jar, and cover with filtered water. Do not fill to the top. It's good practice to leave around ¾ inch (2 cm) between the top of the brine and the lid. If you are using weights, they will raise the brine level, so leave a space closer to 1½ inches (4 cm) or more. Add salt and place the lid on top. Slowly turn your jar from side to side to allow the salt to dissolve. You can also premix your brine and add it in at the same time. Remove the lid and add your weights. Replace the lid and put in a warm corner out of direct sunlight.

When it comes to timing, your ferment will be most active in the first 7 to 14 days. This is when you need to keep a close eye on it and release the bubbles daily. After 14 days, you can taste the liquid to see how the flavor is developing. If you like it, it's done! If not, allow it to keep fermenting and move to the next step once it's to your liking.

When your ferment is ready, drain the contents separating the liquid from the solids. Add the peppers, onion, and garlic to a high-speed blender along with the apple cider vinegar and half the amount of brine. Blend for 2 to 3 minutes on medium speed. Taste your hot sauce to see if it needs any more apple cider vinegar. If your sauce is too thick, add in the other half of the brine. When you reach your desired consistency, add it to your favorite jar or bottle.

STORING
As a rule of thumb, fermented hot sauce will last 2 to 3 months in the fridge, but I've had ones that have lasted an entire year.

Preservation

When it comes to preserving food, there are several ways to extend the life of seasonal produce to use throughout the year. These techniques are often used in meal prep, for homemade camping meals, for pickling cucumbers, and so much more. This section, therefore, will focus on the most common methods used to preserve our food. We'll look at the techniques developed over centuries to prolong the shelf life of produce, ensuring availability and reducing waste. We will explore traditional and modern methods, such as drying, pickling, freezing, and canning, each with its own unique process and application.

Understanding these preservation techniques is essential not only for experts and foodies but also for anyone interested in maximizing food longevity. I'll provide insights into the principles of each method, including the benefits, equipment needed, and the types of food that are best suited for them. Below are some recipes and specific techniques to get you started, from a simple pickling brine to hang drying your own herbs. You will likely find that you already utilize at least one of these preservation methods, and I hope this encourages you to explore a new one. Let's get started with one of the most common methods for preserving and enhancing food: pickling.

Pickling

Pickling involves preserving fruits, vegetables, or other foods by submerging them in a solution of vinegar, salt, sugar, and spices. This process creates a brine that inhibits the growth of bacteria and molds, extending the shelf life of the food while creating new flavors and textures. An example of this is pickled red onions, often used to top dishes to add an acidic element to any meal.

Which Vinegar Should I Choose?

Honestly, it's mostly a matter of preference and taste. I tend to use store-bought apple cider vinegar for red onions because it really enhances their natural sweetness, whereas for jalapeños or cucumbers I usually opt for white distilled vinegar. There are lots of other vinegars, of course, but these are the two that seem to be used the most in pickling.

PICKLED RED ONIONS

5 red onions, sliced thinly

1 cup (237 ml) vinegar

1 cup (237 ml) water

3 tablespoons (54 g) salt

1½ tablespoons (19 g) sugar

/

Yield: 1-quart (1 L) jar

Whether you're pickling cucumbers, red onions, or jalapeños, the fundamental ingredients are simple. You must, however, ensure that whichever vinegar you choose, it is at least 5 percent acidity. This is why it is not recommended to use homemade apple cider vinegar to pickle your vegetables, as the acidity is often lower and unreliable. The following recipe includes a simple brine that you can use to pickle any vegetable, but red onions are a great place to start.

Place the onions in your pickling jar. Add the vinegar, water, salt, and sugar to a saucepan and gently heat over medium heat. When the salt and sugar have dissolved, pour the warm liquid over the red onions, leaving 2 inches (5 cm) of space at the top of the jar. You can use a fermentation weight to keep the onions submerged, but as the jar will be stored in the fridge, this isn't necessary. Add the lid and seal. Once cooled, transfer your jar to the fridge and enjoy your pickles in 24 hours.

NOTE

These can be stored for up to 3 months in the fridge.

VARIATIONS

When pickling veggies, once you've found your perfect ratio, try adding dried herbs, spices, or aromatics. Dill is a favorite of mine, both dried and fresh, to add to pickled veggies or ferments. Garlic, black peppercorns, and mustard seeds will make great additions too. The rule I live by when experimenting is just a little at a time. You don't need a lot, so start with 1 or 2 teaspoons and go from there. As you practice more, you'll get to know the flavors you like best and can adapt any recipe to your liking.

Canning

Canning involves sealing cooked or raw food in airtight containers, typically jars or cans, after they have been heated to kill microorganisms. The jars are first sterilized, and then, once filled, submerged in boiling water. As the jars cool, the lids seal and become shelf stable. This process helps prevent spoilage and allows for long-term storage of various foods, including fruits, vegetables, and soups. Canning helps maintain the quality, flavor, and nutritional value of the preserved food while being an invaluable resource for those seeking to implement self-sufficiency into their life.

Although fairly straightforward once you have the hang of things, there are a few things to be aware of when it comes to canning. There are two main methods: **water bath canning** and **pressure canning**. The method you choose depends on the type of food you're canning, as the acidity of each food is different.

Water bath canning: Water bath canning is suitable for high-acid foods, such as fruits, pickles, jams, and tomatoes. The acidity in these foods helps prevent the growth of harmful bacteria.

Pressure canning: Pressure canning is used for low-acid foods, such as vegetables, meats, poultry, and fish. This method requires a specialized pressure canner for safety.

Regardless of the method you choose, the materials you need are the same and can be found in your regular supermarket, online, or in specialty cooking stores.

1. Canning jars with lids and bands
2. Jar lifter
3. Canning pot or large stockpot with a rack
4. Canning funnel
5. Lid lifter
6. Kitchen towels or cloth
7. Boiling water
8. Acid (e.g., lemon juice or vinegar)
9. Timer
10. Canning recipes for specific foods (check out Ball's book on canning and preserving)

Following canning recipes and guidelines is important to ensure food safety and proper preservation. The exact processing times and procedures may vary depending on the specific food being canned, so always double-check the recipe you're using. Checking seals, getting the level of acidity right, and correctly choosing which method to use prevents the potential of botulism and spoiling your food prep. Canning is a great long-term solution for food preservation, but it takes a little time to get used to all the rules. Once you've grasped them, though, canning will be another tool in your conscious kitchen.

Freezing

Freezing is perhaps the most widely and accessible method of food preservation used by everyone who owns a freezer. There is very little to learn about freezing, and it can be used to preserve almost any fruit, vegetable, or bread. Here are a few things to remember when freezing. Always label your containers so you never forget what you've got stocked away. Include both the name of the food and the date on which it was frozen. To save space, you can always use silicone freezer molds to freeze in specific quantities and then move to a more compact bag system. Although the freezer can be utilized long term, there are some limitations to the time in which you can store things. For example, fruits and vegetables can be stored for around 8 to 12 months, after which they will lose a lot of their flavor and texture and may be unsafe to eat, whereas baked goods are best stored for approximately 3 to 6 months to ensure continued quality. Some items' texture, such as tofu's, will change with freezing. This can be a good thing, unless you're not partial to a slightly spongier tofu texture. My favorite containers to freeze items in are silicone bags because of their pliability. It makes getting the frozen foods out a lot easier.

Freeze-Drying

Freeze-drying, also known as lyophilization, involves removing the moisture from a food or substance by freezing it and then subjecting it to a vacuum environment. This method preserves the food by converting ice directly into water vapor, bypassing the liquid phase. Freeze-drying helps retain the food's original flavor, texture, and nutritional content while making it lightweight and shelf-stable for extended periods, often used in the production of instant coffee and freeze-dried fruits.

Dehydrating

Dehydrating, much like freeze-drying, involves the process of removing water from food. However, dehydrating uses heat, utilizing temperatures ranging from 140°F to 185°F (60°C to 85°C). Yet, hang-drying herbs can be dried at room temperature. For the dehydrating method, you can use your oven, a dehydrator (which can be purchased at most home goods stores), or simply a piece of string in a dark, well-ventilated area.

Drying herbs is an easy way to preserve their flavor and to demonstrate how dehydrating works in its simplest form. Harvest your herbs in the morning before the sun gets too hot and gently wash them to remove any dirt or stragglers. I like to create small bundles of the herbs with a piece of string and hang them upside down in a dry, well-ventilated area. I'm pushed for space, so I just use a clothes hanger and hang the bundles in our cupboard with the door open. Drying time will vary, but a couple of weeks is usually about right. You can give them the "crumble" test to see how far along they are. If they crumble easily, then they're ready; if not, give them another day or two.

The key to successfully drying herbs is good air circulation and low humidity. This method works best for herbs such as rosemary, thyme, lavender, oregano, and sage. Some herbs, such as basil, mint, and cilantro, can be more challenging to dry because they have a higher moisture content, so for these, I'd recommend a dehydrator or oven-drying instead.

Oven-drying is fairly straightforward. You set your oven to the lowest possible temperature setting, ideally between 140°F (60°C) and 170°F (77°C). If your oven does not go this low, keep the door slightly open to lower the temperature. Wash, dry, and thinly spread the herbs (or other food you are drying) on a lined baking tray. Place in the oven, monitoring every few hours, rotating the trays to ensure the produce is dehydrating evenly. This process can take between 6 and 12 hours depending on the moisture content of the food. Once you're satisfied, allow the fruit or veggies to cool completely before storing in an airtight container.

I hope you're feeling a little more confident to experiment in the kitchen with preservation methods and different kinds of ferments. These are fundamental skills to have to create a conscious kitchen and will invariably help you on your sustainable journey. Once you get the hang of the process, making sauerkraut or fermented green tomatoes will feel easy and fulfilling, and ultimately reduce the food wasted in your kitchen.

EATING SEASONALLY IN SPRING

Spring is by far my favorite season. The weather is changing, the crisp mornings are met with the first shoots of the year, and the "hungry gap" is over. Now is the time to start thinking about planting out your summer starts, harvesting the first of the spring greens, and changing up what's on your plate. During the spring season, a variety of fruits and vegetables are available, offering fresh and flavorful options for your meals. We tend to see hardier foods that can survive the colder air while they grow, and perennial plants start to come back and produce for the coming year.

Here's a chart of some common produce that is typically in season during the spring months:

Spring Produce

Fruits	Vegetables	Leafy Greens	Herbs
Apricots: Start to ripen in late spring, offering a sweet-tart flavor	Artichokes: At their peak in spring, great for boiling or steaming	Arugula: Peppery and slightly bitter, perfect for salads, and incredibly easy to grow at home	Basil: A summer favorite for pestos, salads, and topping pizza
Cherries: Begin to come into season in late spring	Asparagus: A springtime favorite, known for its delicate flavor and tender texture	Kale: The leaves are tender in the spring, perfect raw, while later in the year they're better cooked.	Cilantro: A staple in many cuisines, known for its distinctive flavor

Fruits	Vegetables	Leafy Greens	Herbs
Pineapples: Although available year-round, they are at their peak in spring.	Peas: Including snow peas, sugar snap peas, and garden peas	Lettuce: Various types, including romaine, butterhead, and red leaf, are in season.	Dill: An excellent addition to chickpea or potato salads
Rhubarb: Known for its tart flavor, often used in pies or for compote	Radishes: Crisp and peppery, a great addition to salads, and only take 30 days to mature	Swiss chard: The leaves are tender in the spring, perfect raw, while later in the year, they're better cooked.	Mint: Fresh and aromatic, often used in drinks, salads, and desserts
Strawberries: Sweet and juicy, ideal for desserts or as a snack	Spinach: Fresh and tender, ideal for salads		Parsley: Fresh and versatile for garnishing and flavoring
	Spring onions: Milder than regular onions, they add a fresh flavor to salads, curries, tacos, and more.		Sage: An aromatic herb that does well fried or sliced raw

Remember, the availability of these items can vary depending on your location and the local climate. Shopping for seasonal produce not only ensures the freshest flavors but also supports sustainable agriculture and local economies. You'll notice in certain climates that the farmers' markets start up again around springtime, and they're always a good indicator of what's coming into season.

In this chapter, we provide a short collection of plant-based recipes featuring produce that's in season in spring.

Spring Produce Spotlight: Rhubarb

Rhubarb is a perennial plant known for its long, stalk-like stems, which are commonly used in cooking and baking. Rhubarb has large, green leaves and thick, fibrous stalks. The stalks can range in color from green to deep red, depending on the variety, and they have a tart, tangy flavor, which is why they are often sweetened with sugar in recipes and only the stalks of the rhubarb plant are edible.

Rhubarb is commonly used in sweet dishes, such as pies, crumbles, and compotes. It's important not to overcook it to prevent it from turning mushy. Its unique flavor pairs well with ginger, orange, strawberries, and apples.

RHUBARB COMPOTE WITH HOMEMADE SOY YOGURT AND TOASTED NUTS

FOR THE RHUBARB COMPOTE

4 cups (488 g) fresh rhubarb, chopped into 1-inch (3 cm) pieces

½ cup (100 g) sugar (adjust to taste)

¼ cup (60 ml) water

Zest of 1 orange

1 teaspoon vanilla extract

FOR THE HOMEMADE SOY YOGURT (OPTIONAL)

4 cups (946 ml) unsweetened soy milk

2 tablespoons (30 ml) store-bought soy yogurt (as starter culture)

1 tablespoon (15 ml) maple syrup or sugar (optional, for sweetness)

FOR THE TOASTED NUTS

½ cup (45 g) mixed nuts (such as almonds, walnuts, and hazelnuts), roughly chopped

/

Yield: 8 portions

Rhubarb is a wonderful and satisfying plant to grow because you plant it once, and, with care, it will return every year. You can harvest the pink stalks and make an abundance of fresh compote to last all year. This recipe is great for those mornings when you want something light, sweet, and crunchy. This can also be enjoyed as an afternoon snack or a post-dinner dessert.

MAKE THE RHUBARB COMPOTE

In a saucepan, combine the rhubarb, sugar, water, and orange zest. Bring to a boil, then reduce heat and simmer for 10 to 15 minutes until the rhubarb is tender and the mixture has thickened. Remove from heat and stir in the vanilla extract. Allow to cool.

MAKE THE HOMEMADE SOY YOGURT

Heat the soy milk in a saucepan to about 180°F (82°C). Then, let it cool to about 110°F (43°C). Stir in the store-bought soy yogurt and maple syrup or sugar if using.

Transfer the mixture to a yogurt maker or a warm, draft-free place (such as an oven with the light on) for 6 to 12 hours, depending on how thick and tangy you want your yogurt.

Once set, refrigerate the yogurt. You can just use store-bought if pushed for time.

MAKE THE TOASTED NUTS

Preheat the oven to 350°F (175°C). Spread the nuts on a baking sheet and toast for about 8 to 10 minutes, until golden and fragrant. Allow to cool and roughly chop.

To serve, layer the soy yogurt in a bowl, top with a generous amount of rhubarb compote, and sprinkle with toasted nuts. Enjoy for breakfast or a refreshing dessert!

ORZO WITH FRESH HERBY DRESSING AND CRISPY TEMPEH

FOR THE ORZO SALAD

2 cups (400 g) orzo pasta

½ cup (100 g) sun-dried tomatoes, chopped

½ cup (90 g) Kalamata olives, pitted and halved

½ cup (75 g) red onion, finely chopped

1 cup (20 g) arugula or baby spinach

FOR THE FRESH HERBY DRESSING

½ cup (20 g) fresh basil leaves

¼ cup (15 g) fresh parsley leaves

2 tablespoons (8 g) fresh dill

1 garlic clove

Juice of 1 lemon

¼ cup (60 ml) olive oil

Salt and pepper, to taste

FOR THE CRISPY TEMPEH

2 tablespoons (30 ml) soy sauce

1 tablespoon (15 ml) maple syrup

1 teaspoon smoked paprika

8 ounces (227 g) tempeh, sliced into thin strips

Olive oil for frying

/

Yield: 4 portions

This salad is a wonderful blend of flavors and textures—the chewy orzo, tangy sun-dried tomatoes, salty olives, and crispy tempeh are all brought together with the bright herb dressing. It's perfect as a refreshing main dish or a substantial side salad. Enjoy!

MAKE THE ORZO PASTA
Bring a large pot of salted water to a boil. Add the orzo and cook according to package instructions until al dente. Drain and rinse under cold water to stop the cooking process. Set aside.

MAKE THE FRESH HERBY DRESSING
Next, prepare the fresh herby dressing. In a food processor, combine the basil, parsley, dill, garlic, lemon juice, olive oil, salt, and pepper. Blend until smooth. Taste and adjust seasoning if necessary.

MAKE THE CRISPY TEMPEH
In a small bowl, mix the soy sauce, maple syrup, and smoked paprika. Place the tempeh slices in the marinade and let sit for at least 15 minutes. In a skillet, heat the olive oil over medium heat. Add the marinated tempeh and fry until crispy on both sides. Set aside.

In a large bowl, combine the cooked orzo, sun-dried tomatoes, Kalamata olives, red onion, and arugula or baby spinach. Pour the fresh herby dressing over the salad and toss to combine. Divide the salad among serving plates. Top each plate with crispy tempeh slices.

OPTIONAL
Garnish with additional fresh herbs or lemon zest.

Spring Produce Spotlight: Spinach and Arugula

Spinach and arugula are both leafy green vegetables, known for their distinct flavors and nutritional benefits. Spinach has a mild, slightly earthy taste when raw, which becomes more pronounced when cooked. When consumed raw, it's often used in salads, sandwiches, and wraps. When cooked, it's commonly added to soups, stews, sautés, and quiches. It wilts quickly when cooked, reducing in size significantly. I have often used spinach in smoothies or pestos, and its versatility allows it to be baked as well.

Arugula is a leafy green with a peppery, slightly spicy flavor. It has small, tender leaves and is often found in salad mixes. If harvested young, arugula and spinach should be ready to harvest 6 to 8 weeks after sowing. Spinach is a hardy green, so it can be ready in early spring.

ZUCCHINI AND SWISS CHARD VEGAN FRITTATA

14 ounces (397 g) firm tofu (drained and pressed)

¼ cup (88 g) nutritional yeast

½ cup (46 g) chickpea flour (gram flour)

½ cup (118 ml) plant-based milk

½ teaspoon turmeric powder (for color)

½ teaspoon black salt (kala namak) (for an eggy flavor or use regular salt)

Black pepper, to taste

2 tablespoons (30 ml) olive oil

2 garlic cloves, minced

1 medium-size zucchini, thinly sliced

2 cups (72 g) Swiss chard, chopped (stems and leaves separated)

1 tablespoon (4 g) fresh herbs (such as basil or parsley), chopped (optional)

/

Yield: 4 portions

This dish is perfect for a brunch, light dinner, or as a protein-rich addition to any meal.

Preheat the oven to 375°F (190°C). In a blender, combine the tofu, nutritional yeast, chickpea flour, plant-based milk, turmeric, black salt, and black pepper. Blend until smooth to create the frittata base. Heat the olive oil in a nonstick, ovenproof skillet over medium heat. Sauté the garlic for 1 minute until fragrant. Add the zucchini and the stems of the Swiss chard. Sauté until the zucchini is slightly soft and the chard stems are tender, about 5 to 7 minutes. Add the Swiss chard leaves and cook until they just begin to wilt. Pour the blended tofu mixture over the vegetables in the skillet. Stir gently to distribute the vegetables evenly.

Cook on the stovetop for about 5 minutes until the edges begin to set. Transfer the skillet to the preheated oven and bake for 20 to 25 minutes, or until the frittata is firm and the top is slightly golden. Remove from the oven and let it cool for a few minutes. Garnish with fresh herbs before serving.

Slice and serve this delicious vegan frittata warm.

SPRING GARDEN PASTA

FOR THE HOMEMADE KALE PASTA

1 cup (67 g) kale, blanched and pureed

2 cups (240 g) all-purpose flour, plus more for dusting

1 cup (237 ml) water

FOR THE CREAMY PEA, BASIL, AND GARLIC SAUCE

2 tablespoons (30 ml) olive oil

3 garlic cloves, minced

1 small onion, finely chopped

2 cups (330 g) fresh or frozen peas

½ cup (118 ml) vegan cream

1 teaspoon white miso paste

½ cup (20 g) fresh basil leaves

Salt and pepper, to taste

Grated vegan Parmesan cheese, for serving (optional)

/

Yield: 4 portions

This dish combines the earthiness of kale pasta with the freshness of a creamy pea and basil sauce, creating a wonderfully flavorful and satisfying meal. The homemade pasta adds a special touch to the dish, making it perfect for a comforting dinner.

MAKE THE HOMEMADE KALE PASTA

Blanch the kale in hot water for 30 seconds, then immediately place in ice water to stop the cooking process. Squeeze out the excess water. In a blender or food processor, puree the blanched kale until smooth. On a clean surface, make a mound with the flour and create a well in the center. Add the kale puree and half the water. Gradually mix the flour into the water and kale, kneading until a smooth dough forms. Add more water if necessary. Place a glass bowl or wet tea towel over the dough and let it rest for 30 minutes. After resting, roll out the dough nice and thinly, and cut it into your desired pasta shape (e.g., fettuccine, tagliatelle). Bring a pot of salted water to a boil and cook the pasta until al dente, about 2 to 3 minutes. Drain and set aside.

MAKE THE CREAMY PEA, BASIL, AND GARLIC SAUCE

In a saucepan, heat the olive oil over medium heat. Add the garlic and onion and sauté until translucent. Add the peas and cook for a few minutes until they are heated through (or thawed, if using frozen). Stir in the cream and miso paste and bring the mixture to a simmer. Add the basil leaves, salt, and pepper. Cook for an additional 2 to 3 minutes. For a smoother sauce, you can blend the mixture at this point or leave it as is for more texture.

Toss the cooked kale pasta with the creamy pea sauce until well coated. Serve the pasta hot, garnished with grated vegan Parmesan cheese and additional basil leaves, if desired.

Spring Produce Spotlight: Garden Peas

Garden peas, also known as green peas or English peas, are small, sweet, edible seeds that grow inside pods on the *Pisum sativum* plant. They are a type of legume and are different from other varieties such as snow peas or snap peas (see section on peas in the chapter on summer recipes, page 76), where the entire pod is consumed. Garden peas are known for their sweet flavor and starchy texture, which is why they are often enjoyed fresh. Garden peas are a cool-season crop. Their peak season is in the spring, typically from April to June. Fresh garden peas are best when they are young and tender. As they mature, they can become starchy and less sweet.

Fresh peas should be stored in the refrigerator and used relatively quickly, as they can lose their sweetness over time. Dried peas, such as split peas, have a longer shelf life and are used differently in cooking, typically requiring soaking and longer cooking times.

Spring Produce Spotlight: Asparagus

Asparagus is a popular perennial vegetable known for its distinct, slender spears that are harvested in the spring and early summer. Asparagus spears are tall and thin with a pointed tip, which is the bud of the plant. The spears can vary in color, with the most common being green, but there are also white (which is grown underground to prevent chlorophyll development) and purple varieties. Asparagus has a unique, slightly grassy, sweet flavor, and the texture varies depending on the thickness of the spears and how it's cooked—it can be crunchy when lightly cooked or tender when more fully cooked.

Asparagus has a relatively short growing season, typically from April to June, depending on the climate. And if growing your own, it takes around 3 years to see any sizable growth. The peak season for asparagus is in the spring; this is when it's at its best in terms of flavor and texture.

Asparagus is a delicate and versatile ingredient in the kitchen. It can be used as a side dish, in salads, as part of pasta dishes, in risottos, and in soups. It's also commonly served as an appetizer, often simply prepared with olive oil, salt, and pepper. Fresh asparagus should be stored in the refrigerator. To extend its freshness, it can be kept upright in a container with a little water (like flowers in a vase) or wrapped in a damp paper towel and placed in a plastic bag.

CRISPY MISO-BUTTER TOFU WITH ASPARAGUS AND SAUTÉED GREENS

FOR THE CRISPY MISO-BUTTER TOFU

2 tablespoons (32 g) white miso paste

2 tablespoons (28 g) unsalted vegan butter, melted

1 tablespoon (15 ml) soy sauce

1 tablespoon (15 ml) maple syrup or honey

1 tablespoon (15 ml) sesame oil

½ teaspoon garlic powder

14 ounces (397 g) firm tofu, pressed and cut into cubes

Olive oil, for frying

FOR THE ASPARAGUS AND SAUTÉED GREENS

1 pound (454 g) asparagus, trimmed and cut into 2-inch (5 cm) pieces

2 garlic cloves, minced

2 cups (85 g) mixed greens (such as spinach, kale, or chard), roughly chopped

Salt and pepper, to taste

Sesame seeds, for garnish

/

Yield: 4 portions

This dish combines the savory flavors of miso and butter with the crispiness of tofu and the freshness of asparagus and greens. It perfectly balances the nutty depth of miso and melted butter against the crisp, golden tofu. Paired with the earthy crunch of asparagus and the tender sautéed greens, it's full of flavors and textures perfect for a spring afternoon.

MAKE THE CRISPY MISO-BUTTER TOFU

In a bowl, whisk together the miso paste, melted butter, soy sauce, maple syrup, sesame oil, and garlic powder. Add the tofu cubes and gently toss to coat them in the marinade. Let the tofu marinate for at least 15 minutes.

Heat the olive oil in a large skillet over medium-high heat. Add the marinated tofu cubes in a single layer (work in batches if needed). Fry until all sides are golden and crispy, about 3 to 4 minutes per side. Remove from the skillet and set aside.

MAKE THE ASPARAGUS AND SAUTÉED GREENS

In the same skillet, add a bit more olive oil if needed. Add the asparagus and sauté for about 3 to 4 minutes until they start to soften. Add the garlic and sauté for another minute. Add the mixed greens and cook until they are wilted and tender, about 2 to 3 minutes. Season with salt and pepper to taste.

On a serving platter, arrange the sautéed asparagus and greens. Top with the crispy miso-butter tofu. Garnish with sesame seeds.

GRILLED ASPARAGUS WITH MARINATED CHARRED TOFU SKEWERS AND LEMON AND HERB DRESSING

FOR THE TOFU SKEWERS

2 tablespoons (30 ml) soy sauce

2 tablespoons (30 ml) olive oil

1 tablespoon (15 ml) maple syrup or brown sugar

1 teaspoon smoked paprika

1 teaspoon garlic powder

½ teaspoon ground black pepper

14 ounces (397 g) firm tofu, pressed and cut into cubes

Wooden or metal skewers

FOR THE GRILLED ASPARAGUS

1 pound (454 g) asparagus, trimmed

1 tablespoon (15 ml) olive oil

Salt and pepper, to taste

FOR THE LEMON AND HERB DRESSING

Juice and zest of 1 lemon

¼ cup (60 ml) olive oil

1 tablespoon (4 g) chopped fresh parsley

1 tablespoon (2.5 g) chopped fresh basil

1 garlic clove, minced

Salt and pepper, to taste

/

Yield: 4 portions

This dish offers a combination of flavors and textures—the smoky and crispy tofu, tender grilled asparagus, and bright herb dressing. It's perfect for a light meal, especially in the warmer months.

MAKE THE TOFU SKEWERS

In a bowl, whisk together the soy sauce, olive oil, maple syrup, smoked paprika, garlic powder, and black pepper. Add the tofu cubes to the marinade, ensuring they are well-coated. Let them marinate for at least 30 minutes, or longer for more flavor. My preference is 2 hours. Thread the marinated tofu cubes onto skewers. If using wooden skewers, soak them in water for 30 minutes before use to prevent burning.

MAKE THE GRILLED ASPARAGUS

Preheat the grill or grill pan to medium-high heat. Toss the asparagus with the olive oil, salt, and pepper. Grill the tofu skewers and asparagus, turning occasionally, for about 5 to 7 minutes. The tofu should be charred and crispy on the edges, and the asparagus should be tender and slightly charred.

MAKE THE LEMON AND HERB DRESSING

In a small bowl, whisk together the lemon juice, lemon zest, olive oil, parsley, basil, garlic, salt, and pepper.

To serve, arrange the grilled asparagus on a serving platter. Place the tofu skewers on top or alongside the asparagus. Drizzle the lemon and herb dressing over the grilled asparagus and tofu skewers. Serve additional dressing on the side, if desired.

GRILLED ASPARAGUS WITH MARINATED
CHARRED TOFU SKEWERS AND LEMON
AND HERB DRESSING

SPRING RISOTTO WITH FRESH PEAS

1 cup (165 g) fresh peas (or frozen if fresh are not available)

2 tablespoons (30 ml) olive oil

1 small onion, finely chopped

2 garlic cloves, minced

1½ cups (296 g) Arborio rice

½ cup (118 ml) dry white wine (optional)

4 cups (946 ml) vegetable broth, kept warm on the stove

Juice and zest of 1 lemon

2 tablespoons (28 g) unsalted vegan butter (or use additional olive oil)

¼ cup (24 g) vegan Parmesan cheese, grated (optional, can be omitted)

Salt and pepper, to taste

Fresh herbs (such as parsley or basil), chopped, for garnish

/

Yield: 4 portions

This risotto is creamy, comforting, and bursting with the fresh flavors of peas and lemon, making it a perfect dish for spring.

If using fresh peas, blanch them in boiling water for about 1 minute, then drain and set aside. If using frozen, simply thaw them.

In a large skillet or saucepan, heat the olive oil over medium heat. Add the onion and cook until translucent, about 5 minutes. Add the garlic and cook for another minute. Add the rice to the skillet. Stir to coat the grains with oil and toast them slightly for about 2 minutes. This helps to release the starches. Pour in the white wine, if using, and stir until it is mostly absorbed by the rice.

Begin adding the warm vegetable broth one ladle at a time, stirring frequently. Wait until each addition of broth is almost fully absorbed by the rice before adding the next. Continue this process until the rice is creamy and cooked to al dente (this usually takes about 18 to 20 minutes).

When the risotto is just about done, stir in the fresh peas, lemon zest, and lemon juice. Cook for an additional 2 to 3 minutes, or until the peas are heated through. Remove the skillet from heat and stir in the butter and grated Parmesan cheese until well combined. This step adds a rich creaminess to the risotto. Taste and adjust the seasoning with salt and pepper. Serve the risotto immediately, garnished with fresh herbs and additional lemon zest, if desired.

Produce Spotlight: Parsley

Parsley is a popular herb widely used in various cuisines around the world. It belongs to the family *Apiaceae* and is known for its bright green color and fresh, slightly peppery flavor. There are two main types of parsley: curly leaf parsley, known for its ruffled leaves, which is often used as a garnish due to its decorative appearance, and flat-leaf parsley (Italian parsley), which has flat, serrated leaves and is preferred in cooking for its more robust flavor.

Parsley has a fresh, clean, and crisp flavor, albeit a less assertive flavor than other herbs, making it versatile in various dishes. Parsley is a cool-weather herb. It can be grown year-round in milder climates but typically thrives in spring and fall.

Fresh parsley should be stored in the refrigerator. It can be kept in a jar of water, much like cut flowers, and should last for several weeks. You also can dry fresh parsley, though this method reduces the potency of its flavor quite a lot.

CHAPTER

5

EATING SEASONALLY IN SUMMER

The joys of summer are unmatched. Flowers are in full bloom, and all your hard work from late winter into spring finally comes to fruition. Just like the other seasons, the summer months offer an opportunity to change our diets and adopt a lighter, more abundant meal plan. I cannot stress enough how different the flavors of certain foods are when they're picked at the right time, having been allowed to ripen on the vine. Cherry tomatoes are a great example of this. They were the first plants I successfully grew both in Sussex and in Denver, and the flavor was exquisite. Learning how to grow an edible garden taught me what true seasonal eating can look like. It helped me to understand when summer foods should be planted and how long they take to mature; which ones are the most labor-intensive plants and which ones are the most hands-off; and, perhaps most importantly, the role that soil health plays in ensuring food production is high, flavorful, and resilient. All of this helped me understand when to harvest or purchase certain foods at their most flavorful.

Summer offers an abundance of fresh produce. This season is known for its huge harvest of fresh fruits and vegetables, meaning that eating seasonally will include a variety of vibrant and fresh ingredients at their peak flavors and nutritional value. Summer eating often involves things such as salads, smoothies, and grilled vegetables that bring a spectrum of colors to the plate. From deep red strawberries and tomatoes to green zucchini and basil, yellow corn, and purple fairy tale eggplant, the variety of foods we suddenly have is not just utterly stunning to look at but also ensures a wide range of healthy vitamins and minerals, essential on a plant-based diet. The lighter meals and longer daylight hours mean we can enjoy our food while the sun warms our faces: picnics in the park, barbecues with friends and family, and al fresco dining.

I am particularly motivated to experiment during this time and end up with hundreds of notes on new fermentations, ratios for pestos, and fun-yet-bizarre concoctions that seem to work. Let's take a look at some of the most common produce that's in season during the summer months.

Enjoy these light and satisfying summer recipes featuring produce that's in season during the warmest months of the year.

Summer Produce

Fruits	Vegetables	Herbs
Berries: strawberries, blueberries, raspberries, and blackberries	Leafy greens: lettuces, spinach, and Swiss chard	Fresh herbs such as basil, cilantro, dill, sage, parsley, chives, and mint also are abundant in summer.
Melons: watermelons, cantaloupes, and honeydews	Nightshades: tomatoes, bell peppers, and eggplants	
Stone fruits: peaches, nectarines, plums, and cherries	Root vegetables: carrots, beets, and radishes	
Tropical fruits: mangoes and pineapples	Squashes: zucchini and yellow summer squash	
Others: grapes, figs, and tomatillos	Others: green beans, cucumbers, chiles, and sweet corn	

The Conscious Kitchen

Summer Produce Spotlight: Peas

Peas are a versatile and widely cultivated vegetable, belonging to the family *Fabaceae*. They come in several varieties, each with unique characteristics, growth habits, and culinary uses. Here's an overview of the types of peas, how they grow, and how they are used:

Snow peas: These are flat-podded peas eaten whole, pod and all.

Snap peas: A cross between garden and snow peas, snap peas have plump pods and are eaten whole. They are crunchy and sweet.

Field peas: These peas are usually dried and split, often used in soups and stews.

Sugar peas: Similar to snap peas, but often sweeter and more tender.

Cowpeas: Known as black-eyed peas, these are used in various cuisines, particularly in the southern US.

Chickpeas: Also known as garbanzo beans, these are commonly used in Middle Eastern and Indian cuisines.

Peas are typically planted in early spring as soon as the soil can be worked. They prefer cooler weather and can tolerate light frosts. They grow best in well-drained, loamy soil with a neutral pH. Peas need full sun to partial shade. Regular watering is necessary, especially once the plants start flowering and developing pods. Tall varieties of peas often require support from trellises or stakes, as they tend to climb, and they should be harvested regularly to encourage more pod production. The timing of the harvest depends on the variety and desired maturity, but a good rule of thumb is to watch for the pods to swell. At this point, you can feel the pods to see how big the peas are and harvest one to check. Depending on the variety, they take around 50 to 70 days to mature.

Garden peas are often boiled or steamed, used in soups, stews, and side dishes. Snow peas and snap peas are commonly used in stir-fries, salads, and as snacks. Field peas and cowpeas are used in soups, stews, and traditional dishes. Chickpeas are used in hummus, curries, salads, and roasted as a snack. Peas are high in fiber, protein, vitamins (especially vitamins C and K), and minerals.

Each type of pea brings its unique flavor and texture to a variety of dishes, making them a popular choice for gardeners and chefs alike. Whether fresh, frozen, or dried, peas add nutritional value and culinary interest to meals.

FRESH PEA AND ZUCCHINI SALAD WITH HOMEMADE FOCACCIA

2 medium-size zucchini

1 cup (165 g) fresh peas (or frozen, thawed)

A handful of fresh mint leaves, finely chopped

2 tablespoons (30 ml) olive oil

Juice of 1 lemon

Salt and pepper, to taste

¼ cup (61 g) crumbled vegan feta cheese (optional)

2 tablespoons (18 g) pine nuts or slivered almonds (optional)

/

Yield: 2 portions

Making focaccia is a great way to bulk up any meal and add a little more substance. This fresh pea salad highlights the sweetness of garden peas and light crunch of zucchini and is accompanied by fresh herbs and a light vinaigrette to showcase the first veggies of summer.

Using a vegetable peeler or a spiralizer, create thin ribbons or spirals of the zucchini. Place them in a large mixing bowl. If using fresh peas, blanch them in boiling water for 2 to 3 minutes until just tender, then plunge into ice water to retain their bright color. Drain well. If using frozen peas, ensure they are fully thawed.

Add the peas to the bowl with the zucchini ribbons. Toss in the chopped mint. In a small bowl, whisk together the olive oil, lemon juice, salt, and pepper. Adjust the seasoning to your taste. Pour the dressing over the zucchini and peas, and toss gently to coat everything evenly.

If using, sprinkle the crumbled feta and nuts over the top for added flavor and texture. Let the salad chill in the fridge for at least 30 minutes before serving. This allows the flavors to meld together. Serve with focaccia and your preferred protein.

Cont. →

NO-KNEAD FOCACCIA

3 cups (515 g) white
bread flour

2 teaspoons coarse
sea salt

1 teaspoon Italian
seasoning

1¼ tablespoons (28 g)
dry active yeast

1¾ cups (415 ml)
warm water

Olive oil

/

Yield: 1 loaf

Add all the dry ingredients to a mixing bowl and combine. Add the warm water and mix until it forms a wet dough. Cover with a damp cloth or lid and allow to sit for 30 minutes. Perform one round of stretch-and-folds. Replace the lid and move to the fridge to rise overnight, around 18 to 24 hours. Remove from the fridge and allow 2 hours for the dough to come to room temperature. Prepare a baking tray lined with parchment paper. Lightly oil your hands and grab the dough on each side, pulling upward to create a bridge. Then allow the dough to fold underneath itself. Keeping the top of the dough facing upward, move the dough to your lined baking tray. Cover and allow to rise until it fills the tray.

Preheat the oven to 425ºF (218ºC) and lightly oil your hands. Using your fingers, create dimples throughout your dough. Sprinkle sea salt on top and a drizzle of olive oil. Bake for 30 minutes. When the time is up, check the color of your focaccia. If it's still a light brown, bake for an additional 5 minutes. Color equals flavor.

Remove from the baking tray, and allow to cool on a wire rack for 1 hour.

THE PERFECT POTATO SALAD WITH CHIVE FLOWERS, PICKLED RED ONION, AND MUSTARD

1½ pounds (about 700 g) small new potatoes or baby potatoes

3 tablespoons (33 g) Dijon mustard

2 tablespoons (30 ml) extra-virgin olive oil

1 tablespoon (15 ml) apple cider vinegar

1 teaspoon honey or vegan alternative (or to taste)

Salt and pepper, to taste

½ cup (40 g) pickled red onions, thinly sliced

¼ cup (4 g) chive flowers, lightly chopped (reserve a few whole for garnish)

Fresh parsley, chopped (for garnish)

/

Yield: 8 portions

If you usually opt for a store-bought potato salad, then it's time to try making it at home. The perfect potato salad is an excellent accompaniment to any summer picnic or barbecue. It can be made ahead and altered easily to fit your tastes and what you have available. Try substituting Dijon mustard for whole grain for a more interesting visual.

Clean the potatoes and boil them in salted water until they are just tender, about 15 to 20 minutes depending on their size. Drain them and let them cool slightly. If they are larger, you might want to cut them into halves or quarters. In a small bowl, whisk together the Dijon mustard, olive oil, apple cider vinegar, and honey. Season with salt and pepper. Taste and adjust the seasoning or sweetness as needed.

Place the slightly cooled potatoes in a large bowl. Add the red onion. Pour the dressing over the potatoes and onions while they are still warm. Toss gently to ensure all the potatoes are coated with the dressing. The warm potatoes will absorb the flavors better. Gently fold in the chopped chive flowers, reserving a few for garnish. Allow the potato salad to chill in the refrigerator for at least 1 hour. This helps bring the flavors together.

Before serving, give the salad a gentle stir, check for seasoning, and garnish with fresh parsley and the reserved chive flowers.

FLATBREAD WITH TOMATO CONFIT AND FRESH BASIL

**FOR THE
TOMATO CONFIT**

2 cups (488 g) cherry or
grape tomatoes

6 garlic cloves, peeled
and lightly smashed

A few sprigs fresh thyme

A sprig fresh rosemary

Salt and pepper, to taste

A pinch red pepper flakes
for some heat (optional)

1 cup (237 ml) olive oil
(enough to cover the
tomatoes)

Confit is a French cooking technique that not only preserves food but also enhances its flavor and texture. While it is a time-consuming process, the result is a rich and luxurious dish with deep, concentrated flavors. Confit is traditionally used to preserve meats, though it is now also applied to vegetables and fruits. Vegetables or fruits are prepared and then slowly cooked in a substance that inhibits bacterial growth. For vegetables, this is typically olive oil, and for fruits, a sugar syrup. These can be used as a side dish, in salads, or as a dessert (in the case of fruits).

Tomato confit is a wonderfully flavorful accompaniment; tomatoes are slow cooked in oil, garlic, and herbs until tender. You also can make garlic confit the same way, which is incredibly versatile and long lasting.

MAKE THE TOMATO CONFIT
Preheat the oven to 275°F (135°C). Place the tomatoes, garlic cloves, and herbs in a baking dish. Sprinkle with salt, black pepper, and red pepper flakes (if using). Pour olive oil over the tomatoes until they are just covered. Place the baking dish in the oven and cook for about 1.5 to 2 hours. The tomatoes should be very soft and tender but not falling apart. Once done, remove the dish from the oven and let it cool. Store the tomato confit in a jar, ensuring that the tomatoes are covered with oil. It can be kept in the refrigerator for up to a week.

Tomato confit can be used in various ways: as a spread on toast, mixed into pasta, as a topping for bruschetta, or as an accompaniment to cheese and charcuterie boards. The oil from the confit also makes a delicious dressing for salads or a flavorful drizzle for grilled vegetables.

Cont. →

FOR THE FLATBREAD

2 cups (250 g)
all-purpose flour

1 teaspoon baking
powder

½ teaspoon salt

¾ cup (177 ml) water

2 tablespoons (30 ml)
olive oil (plus extra for
cooking)

A pinch of flaky sea salt

Fresh basil

/

Yield: 4 to 6 portions

MAKE THE FLATBREAD

In a mixing bowl, combine the flour, baking powder, and salt. Add the water and olive oil to the dry ingredients. Mix until a dough begins to form. Knead the dough on a floured surface for 6 to 8 minutes until it's smooth and elastic. Divide the dough into six to eight equal portions, depending on the desired size of your flatbreads. Cover with a damp cloth and allow to rest for 10 minutes. Roll out each portion of dough into a thin circle, about ⅛-inch (3 mm) thick. Heat a little olive oil in a frying pan or skillet over medium heat. Cook each flatbread for about 2 to 3 minutes on each side or until it's golden and puffed up. Place the cooked flatbreads on a plate and cover them with a clean towel to keep them warm.

Top your flatbread with tomato confit, flaky salt, and torn pieces of fresh basil. Serve immediately. This dish is great for a light snack or as a starter. You can also build out this meal to be more substantial by adding grilled vegetables or tempeh and salad greens.

 NOTE

Store the tomato confit in an airtight container in the fridge for up to 3 months. The oil should cover the tomatoes while in the fridge and will preserve it.

BBQ TEMPEH BURGER WITH HOMEMADE SLAW

FOR THE BURGERS

8 ounces (227 g) tempeh

½ cup (118 ml) BBQ sauce (see recipe)

4 burger buns

4 lettuce leaves

4 tomato slices

4 red onion slices

2 tablespoons (30 ml) olive oil

Salt and pepper, to taste

FOR THE BBQ SAUCE

1 cup (240 g) tomato ketchup

¼ cup (60 ml) apple cider vinegar

¼ cup (60 g) brown sugar

2 tablespoons (30 ml) honey, or vegan alternative

1 tablespoon (15 ml) vegan Worcestershire sauce

1 teaspoon smoked paprika

½ teaspoon garlic powder

½ teaspoon onion powder

1 tablespoon (11 g) mustard (Dijon or yellow)

½ teaspoon liquid smoke (optional)

½ teaspoon salt

¼ teaspoon black pepper

¼ teaspoon cayenne pepper (optional, for heat)

Tempeh is the perfect substitute to add to your burger. Its light, nutty texture takes on flavors well and can be crisped up to add texture. Together with the mixture of BBQ sauce, homemade slaw, and tempeh, this meal offers the perfect veggie-friendly option.

MAKE THE BURGERS

Slice the tempeh into ½-inch (1 cm)-thick patties. Marinate the tempeh patties in BBQ sauce for at least 30 minutes. Heat the olive oil in a pan over medium heat. Cook the tempeh patties for 3 to 4 minutes on each side, until crispy and browned. Season with salt and pepper to taste. Toast the burger buns lightly. Assemble the burgers with a lettuce leaf, a slice of tomato, a tempeh patty, a slice of red onion, and additional BBQ sauce, if desired.

Serve the BBQ tempeh burger with a side of the homemade slaw.

MAKE THE BBQ SAUCE

In a medium-size saucepan, combine all the ingredients. Stir well to ensure everything is fully mixed. Place the saucepan over medium heat and bring the mixture to a simmer. Reduce the heat to low and let the sauce simmer gently for 20 to 30 minutes. Stir occasionally to prevent sticking or burning. Taste the sauce and adjust seasoning if necessary. For a spicier sauce, you can add more cayenne pepper. Once the sauce has thickened to your desired consistency, remove it from the heat. Let the sauce cool down before using. It can be used immediately or stored in the refrigerator for up to a week.

Cont. ➔

FOR THE HOMEMADE SLAW

2 cups (200 g) cabbage (green and purple), shredded

1 cup (110 g) carrots, shredded

½ cup (115 g) mayonnaise (vegan if preferred)

2 tablespoons (30 ml) apple cider vinegar

1 tablespoon (13 g) sugar

Salt and pepper, to taste

/

Yield: 4 portions

MAKE THE HOMEMADE SLAW

In a large bowl, combine the shredded cabbage and carrots. In a small bowl, whisk together the mayonnaise, apple cider vinegar, sugar, salt, and pepper. Pour the dressing over the cabbage and carrots, and toss well to coat. Let the slaw sit for about 15 minutes before serving to allow the flavors to meld.

The Conscious Kitchen

SWEET CHILI SAUCE

1 cup (237 ml) water

1 cup (237 ml) rice vinegar

1 cup (200 g) sugar

4–5 red chili peppers, finely chopped (adjust according to heat preference)

4 garlic cloves, minced

2 tablespoons (16 g) fresh ginger, grated

2 tablespoons (16 g) cornstarch (optional)

2 tablespoons (30 ml) cold water (for cornstarch slurry)

Salt to taste

/

Yield: 16-ounce (473 ml) jar

Creating a homemade sweet chili sauce with ginger is a great way to use up those extra chiles from the garden or brighten dishes with some sweet and spicy elements. This recipe is simple, flavorful, and has the perfect balance of sweetness, spice, and the zesty kick of ginger.

In a saucepan, combine the water, rice vinegar, and sugar. Stir over medium heat until the sugar dissolves.

Add the chili peppers, garlic, and ginger to the saucepan. Bring the mixture to a boil, and then reduce the heat and simmer for about 10 minutes. In a small bowl, mix the cornstarch with the cold water to create a slurry. Slowly pour this into the simmering sauce while stirring continuously. Keep stirring until the sauce thickens. This should take about 2 to 3 minutes.

Taste the sauce and adjust the seasoning with salt if needed. Remove from the heat and let the sauce cool down. As it cools, the sauce will thicken further. For a smoother sauce, strain it to remove the chili pieces, garlic, and ginger bits. This step is optional and based on personal preference.

NOTE

Once cooled, transfer the sauce to a clean bottle or jar. It can be stored in the refrigerator for up to 2 weeks.

Summer Produce Spotlight: Chiles

Chiles are known for their spicy flavor and varying heat levels. There are numerous varieties, each with unique characteristics, names, and appliances.

Bell pepper: Not spicy and very mild, often used in salads and cooking for their sweet flavor.

Jalapeño: A medium spicy chili commonly used in Mexican cuisine.

Serrano pepper: Similar to jalapeños but smaller and hotter, used in salsas and sauces.

Cayenne pepper: Long, thin, and moderately hot, often dried and ground into powder.

Habanero: Small, lantern-shaped, and very hot, used in hot sauces and spicy dishes.

Ghost pepper: One of the hottest chiles in the world, used sparingly in dishes and sauces.

Scotch bonnet: Similar in heat to habaneros, common in Caribbean cuisine.

Poblano: Mild heat, often stuffed or used in mole sauces.

Thai chili: Small but very spicy, widely used in Southeast Asian cuisine.

Carolina reaper: Currently the hottest chili in the world, used in extremely spicy dishes.

Chiles can be grown from seeds and are typically started indoors and transplanted outside after the last frost. They prefer well-drained, fertile soil with a pH of 6.0 to 6.8. Chiles need full sun for optimal growth. Regular watering is important, but the soil should not be waterlogged. Warm temperatures are necessary, ideally between 70°F and 85°F (21°C to 29°C). Chiles are harvested when they reach the desired size and color, which, depending on the climate, is usually between July and September. The ripening stage can affect the heat level and flavor. For me, some of the easiest and most rewarding chiles to grow have been jalapeños, cayenne, and Scotch bonnet.

HOMEMADE BAKED BEANS (ENGLISH STYLE) WITH ROSEMARY AND SEA SALT BREAD

2 cups (260 g) dried navy beans (or haricot beans)

Olive oil

1 large onion, finely chopped

2 garlic cloves, minced

3 tablespoons (48 g) tomato paste

2 tablespoons (30 g) dark brown sugar

2 tablespoons (30 ml) Worcestershire sauce

1 tablespoon (15 ml) apple cider vinegar

1 teaspoon mustard powder

1 teaspoon smoked paprika

1 14-ounce (400 g) can chopped tomatoes

4 cups (946 ml) vegetable stock or water

Salt and pepper, to taste

/

Yield: 4 to 6 portions

Homemade baked beans are wonderfully comforting and much more flavorful than canned versions. They are perfect on buttered toast, as part of a traditional English breakfast, or as a hearty side dish. This recipe is quite versatile, and you can adjust the sweetness and spices to your liking.

Rinse the beans and soak them overnight in plenty of cold water. This reduces cooking time and makes them easier to digest. Drain and rinse the soaked beans. Place them in a large pot, cover with fresh water, and bring to a boil. Reduce the heat and simmer for about 1 hour or until the beans are tender. Drain and set aside. In a large oven-proof pot or Dutch oven, heat a little olive oil over medium heat. Add the onion and garlic and cook until softened. Add the tomato paste, brown sugar, Worcestershire sauce, apple cider vinegar, mustard powder, and smoked paprika. Cook for another 2 minutes, stirring frequently.

Add the cooked beans to the pot with the sauce. Pour in the tomatoes and vegetable stock. Stir well to combine. Preheat the oven to 300°F (150°C). Cover the pot with a lid and place it in the oven. Bake for 2 to 3 hours, stirring occasionally, until the sauce is rich and thickened. If the beans seem too dry during cooking, add a little more water or stock.

Remove from the oven and season with salt and pepper to taste. Let the beans cool slightly; they will thicken up a bit more as they cool. Serve the baked beans warm.

NO-KNEAD ROSEMARY AND SEA SALT BREAD

4½ cups (617 g) white bread flour (or wholemeal)

1½ cups (355 ml) warm water (give or take)

1½ teaspoons coarse sea salt

2 tablespoons (7 g) dried rosemary

½ teaspoon dried yeast

/

Yield: 1 loaf

Put all the ingredients in a bowl and mix just enough to form a wet dough. Cover with a damp cloth and set aside for 30 minutes on the counter. Then move it to the fridge to rise overnight for 12 to 18 hours.

Preheat the oven to 425ºF (218ºC) and place your pot in the oven for 30 minutes. Lightly flour a surface and turn your dough out, with the underside facing up. Pull the corners of your dough out a little, then fold the left side into the middle, followed by the right side. Then roll your dough from the bottom until the top of the dough is now back on top. Gently form it into a more round ball-like shape. Place on a baking sheet.

Remove the hot pan from the oven carefully, and remove the lid and lift your dough into the pan. Replace the lid and bake for 30 minutes. Then remove the lid and cook for another 12 to 15 minutes. Remove and leave to cool on a wire rack for about an hour.

Store in a brown paper bag or tea towel to preserve freshness. It can also be frozen if you want to bake a few loaves for the month.

Summer Produce Spotlight: Tomatoes

Tomatoes come in all different shapes, sizes, colors, and varieties. Homegrown or in season farmers' market tomatoes just hit differently. Their colors will amaze you, and no doubt their price will too. Tomatoes are quite needy plants, but once you've grasped the basics, they're an incredibly satisfying food to produce at home.

Cherry tomatoes are small, round, and sweet. They're perfect for salads, snacking, and garnishing, and grow in clusters. These are perhaps the easiest and most rewarding variety to grow due to their reputation for prolific yields.

Grape tomatoes are similar to cherry tomatoes but more oblong in shape. They're sweet and firm, making them ideal for salads and snacking.

Heirloom tomatoes are varieties that have been passed down over generations. They come in various sizes, shapes, and colors and are known for their rich, complex flavors. They're great for sandwiches, salads, and eating raw.

Beefsteak tomatoes are large and meaty. These tomatoes are perfect for slicing and using in sandwiches or burgers. They have a classic tomato flavor and are often used in cooking as well.

Roma tomatoes, also known as plum tomatoes, are oval-shaped and have fewer seeds. They are meaty and have a rich flavor, making them ideal for sauces, pastes, and canning.

Campari tomatoes are slightly larger than cherry tomatoes and are known for their juiciness and sweet flavor. They're great for snacking, salads, and cooking.

Green tomatoes, or unripe tomatoes, are firm and tart. If the growing season is particularly short, green tomatoes are harvested before the first frost and left to ripen on windowsills, wrapped in newspapers, or turned into condiments such as chutney or relish.

The perfect time to harvest any tomato is when it's reached its peak color. If you pick them before the entire tomato has fully turned, it will lack the punchy flavor homegrown tomatoes are known for. When it comes to green tomatoes, you don't want to pick them before they've fully developed in size. Unfortunately, this means many will go to the compost if they do not develop before the first frost. You're looking for full-size tomatoes that are still green.

TUSCAN-INSPIRED GRILLED VEGETABLE AND FRESH MIXED TOMATO PANZANELLA

FOR THE GRILLED VEGETABLES

1 medium-size zucchini, sliced lengthwise

1 medium-size yellow squash, sliced lengthwise

1 red bell pepper, seeded and cut into large pieces

1 eggplant, sliced into rounds

Olive oil, for brushing

Salt and pepper, to taste

A few sprigs of fresh thyme or rosemary

FOR THE PANZANELLA

4 cups (360 g) day-old crusty bread (such as ciabatta or sourdough), torn into bite-size pieces

¼ cup (60 ml) extra-virgin olive oil

2 tablespoons (30 ml) balsamic vinegar

1 garlic clove, minced

Salt and pepper, to taste

4 cups (800 g) mixed tomatoes, chopped into bite-size pieces

½ red onion, thinly sliced

Handful of fresh basil leaves, torn

/

Yield: 4 to 6 portions

Panzanella has a beautiful history of using up stale bread and an array of vegetables to prevent waste, and this recipe is no different. This version calls upon the best of summer vegetables and fresh tomatoes while keeping the bread the star of the show. This is a great make-ahead dish that you can bring to any summer event.

MAKE THE GRILLED VEGETABLES

Preheat the grill to medium-high heat. Brush the zucchini, squash, bell pepper, and eggplant with olive oil and season with salt, pepper, and fresh herbs. Grill the vegetables until they are tender and have nice grill marks, about 3 to 4 minutes per side. Once done, let them cool slightly and then chop into bite-size pieces.

MAKE THE PANZANELLA

In a large bowl, toss the torn bread pieces with a bit of olive oil. You can either grill them for a few minutes for extra crispiness or leave them as is for a softer texture. In a small bowl, whisk together the extra-virgin olive oil, balsamic vinegar, garlic, salt, and pepper. In a large bowl, combine the grilled vegetables, tomatoes, red onion, and grilled/toasted bread. Pour the dressing over the salad and gently toss.

Let the salad sit for about 10 to 15 minutes to allow the flavors to meld and the bread to soak up some of the dressing. Just before serving, sprinkle with the torn basil leaves. Enjoy this refreshing and hearty Tuscan-inspired panzanella as a main dish or as a side to other light meals.

This dish can be made ahead and stored in the fridge overnight. Once prepared, consume within 1 to 2 days.

The Conscious Kitchen

CHICKPEA PASTA SALAD WITH DILL AND FRESH PICKLES

2 15.5-ounce (439 g) cans cooked chickpeas, mashed

1 bag cooked pasta (shells, penne, or spiral)

2 medium-size pickles, diced

¼ cup (16 g) fresh parsley, finely chopped

¼ cup (16 g) fresh dill, finely chopped

1 cup (230 g) mayonnaise

2 tablespoons (30 ml) pickle brine

1 tablespoon (11 g) mustard (Dijon or whole-grain)

Salt and pepper, to taste

Mixed greens (such as spinach, arugula, or lettuce), as desired

/

Yield: 6 portions

Chickpeas are increasingly being used as an alternative to fish, mimicking the flaky texture and protein content. This recipe is a veganized, elevated version of a "tuna salad." With the additions of fresh herbs and pickles, the salad celebrates tangy flavors and the freshness of the summer garden.

In a large mixing bowl, combine the mashed chickpeas and cooked pasta. Add the pickles, parsley, and dill to the bowl. Mix well to distribute the flavors. In a small bowl, whisk together the mayonnaise, pickle brine, and mustard. Season with salt and pepper to taste. Pour the dressing over the chickpea and pasta mixture. Gently toss everything together until well coated. Serve your chickpea salad on a bed of mixed greens. This can be enjoyed as a pasta salad, or you can omit the pasta and use the mixture to make a sandwich.

NOTE

Feel free to add additional ingredients such as chopped or pickled onions, bell peppers, or cherry tomatoes for extra flavor and crunch. Store in the fridge in an airtight container and consume within 3 to 5 days.

EATING SEASONALLY
IN AUTUMN

Autumn ushers in the first cold winds and chilly nights that have us counting down the days until the first frost. For us gardeners, it's time to look at our summer crops and decide when it's time to do our last harvest and prepare for winter. Our meals tend to get a little heavier with the additions of squash, pumpkins, hearty stews, and cozy soups. Once again, our diet changes with the season, as do our gardens and our pantries. Although I adore summer, the following months are full of activity, preparing cabbage for sauerkraut, cucumbers for pickling, and tomatoes for canning. Autumn is truly a time of experimentation, giving us all a chance to play around with new ingredients and methods of cooking. In chapter 3, we discussed the methods for preserving our foods to last through the winter, and all this preservation happens in autumn. So, in this chapter we'll look at what's in season, how to plan for autumn, and lots of recipes to contribute to our conscious kitchens.

Part of keeping a conscious kitchen is preventing waste where possible. In late summer, I think about the ways in which my zero-waste habits change from season to season and how I can apply skills I already have to those habits. For example, summer habits include watering efficiently to keep my plants happy while conserving water or harvesting ripe fruit before it goes bad. As we move into autumn, I think about harvesting fruit, ripe or not, before the first frost and consider ways to use or preserve them. Planning helps me to prevent waste.

To start planning, I ask myself a lot of questions about the foods I enjoy, what preservation skills I can use to prevent waste, what supplies I need, and what produce I can use to make the recipes interesting. Your questions may look different from mine, but it's a wonderful exercise to get you thinking about what needs to be done. Once I've gathered my thoughts, I prioritize the most important tasks and set aside some time to address them.

Helpful to me is front-loading my day with the most time-intensive tasks. I've also found it helpful to keep a calendar specific to my conscious kitchen so that I don't need to hold all these important dates in my head and risk forgetting them.

So, to help with our planning, let's look at what's in season. In autumn, a variety of fruits and vegetables come into season, offering us lots of fresh produce. Here are some common items that are typically in season during autumn.

Autumn Produce

Fruits	Vegetables
Apples: Autumn is prime time for apples, with many varieties reaching their peak.	Beet: An earthy root vegetable, usually found in autumn and available in many varieties. They make an excellent addition to salads and stews and are good pickled too.
Cranberries: They come into season in the fall, just in time for holiday cooking.	Broccoli: Cooler temperatures bring out its best flavors.
Figs: Late summer and early autumn are when figs are typically harvested	Brussels sprouts: They are at their best after the first frost of the season.
Grapes: Late summer and early autumn are when grapes are at their juiciest.	Cauliflower: This versatile vegetable is great in autumn.
Pears: Like apples, pears are a staple fruit of the autumn season.	Kale: Cooler weather enhances its flavor.
Persimmons: These unique fruits are a special treat in the fall.	Squash: Varieties such as butternut, acorn, and spaghetti squash are abundant in autumn.
Pomegranates: Autumn is the season for these jewel-like fruits.	Sweet potatoes: These are at their sweetest and most flavorful in the fall.
Pumpkins: A hallmark of autumn, pumpkins are not just for decoration but are also great in cooking.	

Autumn Produce Spotlight: Mushrooms

Mushrooms are a fascinating and diverse group of fungi with a wide range of types, growing conditions, and uses. Fungi, a distinct kingdom separate from plants, animals, and bacteria, are a diverse group of organisms that play vital roles in many ecological systems. They range from microscopic yeasts to large mushrooms. Unlike plants, fungi don't photosynthesize; they obtain nutrients by absorbing organic matter, often by decomposing dead organisms or as symbionts with plants.

Fungi are found in almost every habitat, from soil and water to living and dead organisms. They're essential to many processes on Earth, including nutrient cycling and the formation of soils. Despite their critical roles, they are often less visible and less studied than plants and animals. If you find the world of fungi as fascinating as I do, I highly suggest reading *The Hidden Life of Trees* by Peter Wohlleben.

The peak season for harvesting mushrooms falls over August, September, and October.

Button: These are the most common variety, often found in grocery stores. They can be white or brown (crimini) and mature into portobellos.

Shiitake: Known for their rich, savory flavor, they are often used in Asian cuisine.

Oyster: These have a delicate texture and a mild, sweet taste.

Enoki: With their long, thin stems and small caps, they are popular in Japanese dishes.

Morel: Highly prized for their honeycomb appearance and nutty flavor, morels are a favorite among gourmet cooks.

Chanterelles: Chanterelles are known for their golden color and fruity, peppery flavor.

Porcini: A staple in Italian cuisine, they are renowned for their meaty texture and earthy flavor.

Truffles: These are highly valuable and known for their intense aroma. They are used in high-end cuisine.

Mushrooms grow from spores, not seeds, and they need specific conditions to thrive. They grow on various organic materials, such as wood, soil, or decaying matter. Each species prefers a different substrate. Mushrooms require a moist environment to develop. Most mushrooms grow best in mild temperatures. While mushrooms don't use photosynthesis, some require light to initiate the fruiting process.

MUSHROOM STOOP WITH PARSLEY DUMPLINGS

FOR THE STOOP

½ cup (60 g) porcini mushrooms

1 tablespoon (15 ml) olive oil

2 tablespoons (28 g) vegan butter

3 medium-size onions, diced

2 medium-size carrots, diced

1 celery stalk, diced

4 garlic cloves, finely chopped

4 cups (500 g) mushrooms, sliced

4¼ cups (1 L) mushroom or vegetable stock

FOR THE DUMPLINGS

Handful of flat leaf parsley, finely chopped

Handful of dill, finely chopped

2–3 tablespoons (30–44 ml) cold water

¾ cup (100 g) self-rising flour

English mustard powder

2 ounces (50 g) vegetable suet

/

Yield: 6 portions

A stoop falls somewhere between a soup and a stew, and it is equal parts hearty and delicious. For this stoop, mushrooms provide the base flavor, enriched by vegetables and homemade dumplings. This recipe is perfect for a cozy night in by the fire.

MAKE THE STOOP

Place the porcini mushrooms in a bowl and cover with hot water. Allow to rehydrate for 30 minutes. Strain the porcini mushrooms and set the liquid aside. Place a heavy-bottomed pan on medium heat and add the olive oil and vegan butter. When the oil is simmering, add the onions, carrots, and celery to the pan and cook for around 10 to 12 minutes with the lid on. Add the garlic to the pan and sauté for 1 to 2 minutes. Add the mushrooms and sauté for 6 to 8 minutes.

Once the porcini mushrooms have softened, add the vegetable stock, strained porcini liquid, and chopped mushrooms and bring to a simmer while you make the dumplings. For a thicker soup, you can blend 1 to 2 cups (237 to 437 ml) of the liquid and return it to the pan.

MAKE THE DUMPLINGS

For the dumplings, finely chop the herbs and add all the dry ingredients to a bowl, mixing thoroughly. Add the cold water a tablespoon (15 ml) at a time and mix until it forms a shaggy dough. You don't want the dumplings to be wet. Make sure to use just enough water to combine. Take around one-eighth of the mixture and form it into a ball. Repeat for the rest of the dough until you have nine to ten dumplings. Uncover the stoop and add the dumplings (they should float). Spoon some of the liquid over them to coat, then replace the lid. Allow to simmer for around 15 minutes.

Serve in a bowl with a large piece of crusty bread.

VEGAN FULL ENGLISH BREAKFAST

1 package (about
12 ounces [340 g]) silken
tofu

2 tablespoons (22 g)
nutritional yeast

½ teaspoon turmeric
(for color)

½ teaspoon garlic powder

½ teaspoon onion powder

Salt and pepper, to taste

1 tablespoon (15 ml) olive
oil or vegan butter

1 small onion, finely
chopped

1 bell pepper, diced (any
color)

1 cup (30 g) spinach or
kale, chopped

¼ cup (28 g) vegan
cheese, diced tomatoes,
sliced avocado, or
chopped herbs for
garnish (optional)

/

Yield: 2 portions

A full English breakfast is a traditional British breakfast known for being very hearty and usually eaten on the weekend, though it can be eaten anytime. It typically includes eggs (fried, scrambled, or poached), traditional British sausages, crispy strips of bacon, baked beans in tomato sauce, buttered toast, grilled or fried tomatoes, fried or grilled mushrooms, hash browns, and tea or coffee. Creating a vegan or even vegetarian version of a full English breakfast is very easy, especially with the availability of alternatives. This vegan full English breakfast will offer the same satisfying and robust experience as the traditional one, but it is entirely plant-based!

SILKEN TOFU SCRAMBLE

Gently press the silken tofu to drain out excess water. Be careful as silken tofu is quite delicate. In a small bowl, mix the nutritional yeast, turmeric, garlic powder, onion powder, salt, and pepper. Heat the olive oil or vegan butter in a nonstick pan over medium heat. Sauté the onion and bell pepper until they are soft and slightly browned.

Crumble the silken tofu into the pan with the veggies. It's okay if it breaks apart; silken tofu is meant to be very soft. Sprinkle the spice mix over the tofu and gently fold it in, trying not to break the tofu too much. Stir in the spinach or kale and cook until the greens are wilted. Taste and adjust the seasoning as needed. If using, stir in vegan cheese at this stage to allow it to melt slightly.

Serve hot, garnished with the tomatoes, avocado, or herbs, if desired. This scramble goes well with toast, in a breakfast burrito, or as a part of a larger brunch spread.

The Conscious Kitchen

HASH BROWNS

4 large potatoes (russet or Yukon gold work well)

½ medium-size onion, finely chopped

2 tablespoons (16 g) all-purpose flour (or a gluten-free alternative)

½ teaspoon garlic powder

½ teaspoon onion powder

¼ teaspoon paprika or cayenne pepper for extra flavor (optional)

Salt and pepper, to taste

2–3 tablespoons (30–44 ml) olive oil or vegetable oil for frying

/

Yield: 2 to 4 portions

Wash and peel the potatoes. Grate them using a box grater or a food processor with a grating attachment. Place the grated potatoes in a bowl of cold water for a few minutes to remove excess starch. Drain the potatoes and squeeze out as much water as possible using a clean kitchen towel or cheesecloth. This step is crucial for crispy hash browns.

In a large bowl, mix together the grated potatoes, onion, flour, garlic powder, onion powder, and optional paprika or cayenne. Season with salt and pepper to taste. Shape the potato mixture into patties. You can make them as large or as small as you like.

Heat the oil in a large skillet over medium-high heat. Once hot, add the hash brown patties.

Cook each side for about 4 to 5 minutes or until they are golden brown and crispy. Be careful not to overcrowd the pan. Once cooked, place the hash browns on a paper towel–lined plate to absorb any excess oil. Serve hot, ideally with a side of vegan sour cream, ketchup, or your favorite sauce.

NOTE

To make your full English breakfast, toast two pieces of rosemary sea salt bread. Butter both pieces and place on a plate. Add a portion of the silken tofu scramble, hearty baked beans, sautéed mushrooms and spinach, one or two veggie sausages, and one or two hash browns. Enjoy with a cup of tea or coffee.

Cont. →

SAUTEED MUSHROOMS AND SPINACH

2 tablespoons (30 ml) olive oil

4 garlic cloves, minced

1 pound (about 450 g) mushrooms, sliced (any variety such as button, cremini, or shiitake)

Salt and pepper, to taste

1 tablespoon (15 ml) soy sauce or balsamic vinegar, or a pinch of red pepper flakes (optional)

4 cups (120 g) fresh spinach leaves

A squeeze of lemon juice for extra flavor (optional)

/

Yield: 4 portions

In a large skillet, heat the olive oil over medium heat. Add the garlic to the skillet. Sauté for about 1 minute, or until fragrant. Be careful not to burn the garlic. Add the mushrooms to the skillet. Cook for about 5 to 7 minutes, or until the mushrooms are golden and have released their moisture. Season the mushrooms with salt and pepper. If you're using soy sauce, balsamic vinegar, or red pepper flakes, add them now.

Add the spinach to the skillet. Cook, stirring occasionally, until the spinach wilts, which should take about 2 to 3 minutes. If desired, add a squeeze of lemon juice for a bit of zest and adjust the seasoning as needed. Serve the sauteed garlic mushrooms and spinach immediately.

Autumn Produce Spotlight: Beets

Beets are a root vegetable scientifically known as *Beta vulgaris*. They are known for their deep red or purple color and distinct sweet, earthy flavor. Beets are used not only for culinary purposes but also for natural dyeing and experimentation.

Typically, beets have a deep red or purple color, but there are also golden and white varieties. The bulbous root part is most commonly eaten, but the green leafy tops are also edible and nutritious. Beets are high in fiber, vitamins (such as folate and vitamin C), minerals (such as potassium and iron), and antioxidants.

Beets are grown from seeds, though you can always purchase starts from your local nursery. They prefer cool temperatures, making them ideal for spring or fall planting in temperate climates. Beets are ready to harvest when they are about the size of a golf ball to a tennis ball, depending on the variety, and are a great beginner-friendly crop. Harvest times vary from 45 to 65 days, and beets can be picked from October to November when planted in the fall. For spring harvests, if planting around 2 weeks before the last frost, these can then be harvested 45 to 65 days later.

They are often roasted or boiled and sliced into salads and sometimes paired with a soft vegan cheese, nuts, and greens. Beets' sweet taste makes them a popular addition to juices and smoothies, with people even claiming they have energizing properties to give you a boost before your next workout. Whether this is true, however, is yet to be determined. They can be pickled with vinegar, sugar, and spices, or used in baking for their natural sweetness and color.

BEET TART WITH ORANGE ZEST

Even for those of you who may shy away from beets, the earthy flavors are delicately balanced with the sweetness of the orange in this recipe, creating a sweet and savory tart. It pairs well with a salad, as part of a picnic, or with freshly steamed vegetables.

FOR THE PASTRY

1⅔ cups (200 g) plain flour

¼ teaspoon salt

½ cup (112 g) cold butter, diced

2–3 tablespoons (30–44 ml) cold water

FOR THE FILLING

2 medium-size beets, peeled and sliced thinly

1 large red onion, sliced

1¼ cups (188 g) vegan feta cheese, crumbled

Fresh thyme or rosemary (optional)

Salt and pepper, to taste

/

Yield: 4 portions

MAKE THE PASTRY

In a large bowl, combine flour and salt. Add the butter and rub into the flour using your fingertips until the mixture resembles breadcrumbs. Gradually add cold water and mix until the dough just comes together. Be careful not to overwork the dough. Form the dough into a disc, wrap in plastic wrap, and chill in the fridge for at least 30 minutes.

Preheat the oven to 375°F (190°C). Roll out the pastry on a lightly floured surface and line a 9-inch (22 cm) tart tin. Prick the base with a fork, line with parchment paper, and fill with baking beans or rice. Bake for 15 minutes, then remove the beans and paper and bake for another 5 minutes until golden.

MAKE THE FILLING

While the pastry is prebaking, gently sauté the beets and red onion in a pan with a little oil until they are just softened. Set aside to cool.

Spread the cooked beets and red onion evenly over the prebaked pastry base. Sprinkle the crumbled feta over the vegetables. If using, sprinkle some fresh thyme or rosemary on top. Bake for 25 to 30 minutes, or until the filling is set and the top is golden.

Let the tart cool for a few minutes before serving. It can be enjoyed warm or at room temperature, with a salad.

SEASONAL CHILI WITH PUMPKIN AND DARK CHOCOLATE

2 tablespoons (30 ml) olive oil

1 large onion, finely chopped

3 garlic cloves, minced

1 bell pepper, diced

1 teaspoon ground cumin

1 teaspoon ground cilantro

½ teaspoon ground smoked paprika

½ teaspoon ground cinnamon

1 medium-size pumpkin, peeled and diced into bite-size pieces

2 cups (360 g) kidney beans (either canned or soaked overnight and boiled)

1 14.5-ounce can (400 g) diced tomatoes

2 cups (473 ml) vegetable broth

3–4 squares of high-quality dark chocolate (70 percent or higher)

Salt and pepper, to taste

1 tablespoon (16 g) miso paste

Juice of half a lime

Fresh cilantro, pickled red onions, 1 tablespoon (15 g) vegan sour cream, and avocado for garnish (optional)

/

Yield: 6 portions

The thing about chili is that it's versatile. So, this recipe lends itself to being adapted where needed to what you have available at home or in the garden. The addition of chocolate and miso add a wonderful depth to this hearty meal, bringing the flavors of a traditional chili to this vegetarian version.

In a large pot, heat the olive oil over medium heat. Add the onion, garlic, and bell pepper. Sauté until the onions are translucent. Stir in the cumin, cilantro, smoked paprika, and cinnamon. Cook for about a minute until fragrant. Add the pumpkin, kidney beans, tomatoes, and vegetable broth to the pot. Stir well to combine. Bring the mixture to a boil, then reduce the heat and let it simmer for about 20 to 25 minutes, or until the pumpkin is tender.

Once the pumpkin is cooked, add the dark chocolate to the chili. Stir until the chocolate is completely melted and incorporated into the chili. Taste and adjust seasoning with salt, pepper, or more spices if needed. Serve hot, garnished with fresh cilantro, pickled red onions, a spoonful of sour cream, and slices of avocado, if desired.

Produce Spotlight: Pumpkins and Squash

Pumpkins and squash are members of the Cucurbitaceae family, which also includes cucumbers, melons, and gourds. They are grown primarily for their edible fruit, though they also have ornamental uses. Once dried, you can carve some varieties of gourds into spoons, sculptures, or even a birdhouse. There are also Luffa, which are grown just like any other squash and left to dry on the vine. You remove the outer skin and the seeds, using what's left as a bathroom sponge. This family of produce is truly remarkable and perhaps one of the most versatile.

Both pumpkins and squash are fruits from a botanical perspective, although they are often used as vegetables in cooking. They come in various shapes, sizes, and colors. There are many types of squash, broadly categorized into summer squash (such as zucchini and yellow squash) and winter squash (such as butternut, acorn, and spaghetti squash). Pumpkins are a type of winter squash but are distinguished by their round shape and orange color.

Pumpkins and squash are typically grown from seeds. They require warm soil and are often planted after the last frost in spring. They thrive in warm, temperate climates and need a lot of sunlight. These plants are vine-growing and need ample space to spread out. They have male and female flowers and usually require bees or other pollinators for fruit production

CREAMY PUMPKIN GNOCCHI WITH VEGGIE SAUSAGE AND SAGE

FOR THE GNOCCHI

2 cups (480 g) pumpkin puree (canned or homemade)

2–2½ cups (250–313 g) all-purpose flour or semolina

1 teaspoon salt

½ teaspoon nutmeg

FOR THE CREAMY SAUCE

1 garlic clove, minced

1 cup (237 ml) canned coconut milk

½ cup (118 ml) vegetable broth

2 tablespoons (22 g) nutritional yeast

Salt and pepper, to taste

FOR THE SAUSAGE AND SAGE

2 tablespoons (30 ml) olive oil

4 vegan sausages, sliced

A handful of fresh sage leaves

/

Yield: 4 portions

Gnocchi is an easy and fun way to get started with homemade pasta. The ingredients are simple, the method is straightforward, and the results are delicious. This recipe is also a great way to use up any leftover pumpkin puree from your seasonal lattes and ensure it doesn't go to waste.

MAKE THE GNOCCHI
Mix the pumpkin puree, flour, salt, and nutmeg in a bowl to form a dough. Add more flour if the dough is too sticky. Knead the dough until smooth, cover with a damp towel, and allow to rest for 10 minutes. On a floured surface, roll the dough into long ropes and cut into small pieces to form gnocchi. Bring a pot of salted water to a boil. Cook the gnocchi in batches until they float to the top, then remove the gnocchi with a slotted spoon.

MAKE THE CREAMY SAUCE
In a pan, heat a bit of oil and sauté the garlic until fragrant. Add the coconut milk, vegetable broth, and nutritional yeast. Simmer until the sauce thickens. Season with salt and pepper.

MAKE THE SAUSAGE AND SAGE
In another pan, heat the olive oil and fry the vegan sausage slices until they are browned and crispy. Add the sage leaves to the pan and fry until crisp.

Toss the cooked gnocchi in the creamy sauce, gently coating each piece. Plate the creamy gnocchi and top with the crispy sausage slices and sage leaves. Optionally, garnish with vegan Parmesan cheese or additional nutritional yeast.

BAKED SQUASH WITH CINNAMON, STAR ANISE, AND HARISSA COUSCOUS

FOR THE BAKED SQUASH

2 medium-size carrots, peeled and cut into chunks

2 parsnips, peeled and cut into chunks

4 red onions, quartered

1 cinnamon stick

2 star anise

3 tablespoons (44 ml) olive oil

Salt and pepper, to taste

½ teaspoon ground ginger

¼ teaspoon ground turmeric

1 serrano pepper

2¼ cups (300 g) butternut squash, peeled and cut into chunks

½ cup (100 g) dried apricots, roughly chopped

1¾ cups (300 g) cooked chickpeas

1¼ cups (300 ml) aquafaba

FOR THE COUSCOUS

1¼ cups (200 g) couscous

1¾ cups (414 ml) vegetable stock, hot

2 tablespoons (30 ml) olive oil

Salt, to taste

2 tablespoons (30 g) Harissa paste

¼ cup (30 g) preserved lemon skin, finely chopped

FOR THE GARNISH

Fresh cilantro

Toasted almonds or pine nuts (optional)

/

Yield: 4 portions

If you're looking for a store cupboard meal that utilizes earthy, autumn root vegetables, then this is it. It combines the flavors traditionally found in North African and Middle Eastern cooking, such as harissa, to add a new dimension to the vegetables and enhance the couscous. Harissa is a spicy and aromatic chili paste commonly used to add heat and flavor to dishes. A staple for any cupboard looking to elevate their meals.

MAKE THE BAKED SQUASH

Preheat the oven to 400°F (200°C). Place the vegetables, except the squash, in a large oven-proof dish. Add the cinnamon stick and star anise, oil, salt, and all the other spices. Mix well and place in the oven and cook for 15 minutes. Add in the squash and bake for an additional 30 minutes. At this point, add the dried apricots, chickpeas, and aquafaba. Return to the oven for an additional 10 minutes.

MAKE THE COUSCOUS

Place the couscous in a large bowl. Pour the hot vegetable stock over the couscous, add the olive oil and a pinch of salt, and stir briefly. Cover the bowl with a lid and let it sit for 10 minutes. Fluff the couscous with a fork. When ready to serve, add the harissa and preserved lemon skin to the couscous and mix.

Spoon the couscous onto a large serving dish. Place the roasted squash and other vegetables on top of the couscous. Garnish with chopped fresh cilantro and toasted almonds or pine nuts, if using.

APPLE AND BLACKBERRY CRUMBLE

FOR THE FILLING

6 medium-size apples, peeled, cored, and sliced

2 cups (288 g) blackberries, fresh

½ cup (115 g) brown sugar

1 teaspoon cinnamon

2 tablespoons (30 ml) lemon juice

1 tablespoon (8 g) cornstarch (to thicken the juices)

FOR THE CRUMBLE TOPPING

1½ cups (188 g) all-purpose flour (use gluten-free if desired)

½ cup (115 g) brown sugar

½ teaspoon ground cinnamon

A pinch of salt

½ cup vegan butter (112 g), cubed, or coconut oil (118 ml)

/

Yield: 6 portions

Creating a vegan apple and blackberry crumble is a delicious and straightforward process that works perfectly as a dessert after your Sunday roast. Blackberries grow on perennial plants with biennial stems called canes. They can be either erect or trailing. They ripen in late summer to early autumn. When ripe, blackberries are soft and deeply colored. There are many varieties, some thornless and some with thorns, with subtle differences in flavor and hardiness. If you've never added blackberries to your apple pie or crumble before, then you're in for a treat. They balance perfectly with the sweetness of the apple, the warming spices of the cinnamon, and the crumble topping.

MAKE THE FILLING

Preheat the oven to 375°F (190°C). In a large mixing bowl, combine the apples, blackberries, brown sugar, cinnamon, lemon juice, and cornstarch. Mix well until the fruit is evenly coated. Pour the fruit mixture into a baking dish, spreading it out evenly.

MAKE THE CRUMBLE TOPPING

In another bowl, mix together the flour, brown sugar, cinnamon, and a pinch of salt. Add the vegan butter or coconut oil to the dry ingredients. Mix until the mixture resembles coarse crumbs. Sprinkle the crumble topping evenly over the fruit mixture in the baking dish.

Place the dish in the preheated oven and bake for about 35 to 45 minutes, or until the topping is golden brown and the fruit mixture is bubbling. Allow the crumble to cool slightly before serving. It can be enjoyed on its own or with a scoop of vegan ice cream or a dollop of vegan whipped cream.

NOTE

This dessert can be made ahead and stored in the fridge or freezer. Make sure to allow the crumble to cool completely before covering and refrigerating or freezing.

Autumn Produce Spotlight: Apples

Apples are one of the most popular and versatile fruits, with a wide range of varieties, each with its own unique taste, texture, and color. They are used in various culinary applications, from eating fresh to cooking and baking. When autumn comes around, it highlights the best of what we can create with apples, from tarts and pies to cakes, compotes, and caramel apples. Although available all year-round, they're at their peak flavor during their true growing season, which falls between August and November depending on the variety.

Red Delicious: Red Delicious are known for their deep red color and sweet flavor, but they are not favored for cooking due to their mealy texture.

Granny Smith: These are bright green, crisp, and tart, excellent for baking and cooking.

Gala: Gala apples are small, with a mild and sweet flavor, suitable for both eating raw and cooking.

Fuji: Fuji apples are sweet and juicy, great for snacking and salads.

Honeycrisp: These are crisp and juicy with a balanced sweet-tart flavor, good for eating fresh and in salads.

Braeburn: Braeburns are crisp and tangy, suitable for both eating raw and cooking.

Golden Delicious: These are sweet and mellow, versatile for both raw consumption and cooking.

McIntosh: McIntosh apples are tart and slightly sweet, with a softer flesh, good for sauces and pies.

Cooking apples are a variety seen mostly in the UK and Europe. They're a larger fruit that tend to have a sour taste with less of the sweetness of other varieties. This is what makes them ideal for baking. Their sharpness pairs well with the sweetness generally added through sugar for dishes such as apple crumble. They have a wonderful texture that breaks down perfectly when stewed before baking. Bakers in the US tend to opt for varieties such as Granny Smith due their tart flavor.

CHAPTER

7

EATING SEASONALLY IN WINTER

Eating seasonally during winter definitely involves a shift in diet to embrace the fresh, local produce that thrives in the colder weather. This approach not only supports local agriculture but also ensures a diet rich in nutrients and flavors specific to this time of year. Despite the colder weather, there are still plenty of fruits and vegetables that come into season during the winter months. Although autumn takes credit for the beginning of squash and pumpkin season, these vegetables persist into winter, and if stored correctly (see page 30), they can last for months.

Root vegetables such as carrots, beets, and turnips become staples, offering both robust flavors and nutrient density. These can be roasted, stewed, or turned into hearty soups and pies, perfect for chillier days. Winter greens such as kale, collards, and Swiss chard are also abundant; their slightly bitter taste complements the richer dishes typical of the season while citrus fruits are definitely a bright spot in winter, providing much-needed vitamin C to help combat the lack of sunshine. Oranges, grapefruits, and lemons can be used in a variety of ways, from fresh salads to warm citrus-infused desserts, and rich lemony risotto.

I also find myself relying heavily on pantry staples, such as grains and legumes, and comforting and filling dishes such as shepherd's pie, warm grain salads, and bean stews. Herbs and spices, such as rosemary, thyme, cinnamon, and nutmeg, also are used more prominently, adding depth and warmth to our favorite dishes. Eating seasonally in winter is not just about the ingredients; it's about the method of cooking as well. Slow cooking and roasting are popular, as they bring out the rich flavors and aromas of the ingredients, making our meals particularly cozy and comforting in the snowy, wet, and gray seasons.

Winter eating is characterized by hearty vegetables, warming spices, and rich slow-cooked dishes. Let's take a look at what's in season and move on to discover some warm and comforting winter recipes.

Winter Produce

Fruits	Vegetables
Apples: Many varieties are still in season, offering sweetness and crunch	Beets: Earthy flavor, great roasted or in salads
	Brussels sprouts: Nutritious and great when roasted
Grapefruits: Another citrus fruit that's both tangy and sweet	Cabbage: Versatile and can be used in various dishes such as stews and salads
Kiwis: Rich in vitamins and a tropical taste	
	Carrots: Sweet and crunchy, ideal for soups, stews, and roasting
Oranges: Rich in vitamin C, perfect for boosting immunity during cold months	
	Kale: A hearty green, great for soups and stews
Pears: Soft, sweet, and great for baking or eating raw	
	Leeks: Add a mild onion-like flavor to dishes
Persimmons: With a unique texture and flavor, they're delicious when fully ripe	
	Sweet potatoes: Rich in fiber and vitamins, excellent for roasting
Pomegranates: Known for their juicy seeds, great in salads or as a snack	
	Turnips: Root vegetables that are versatile in cooking
Tangerines: Smaller and sweeter than oranges, easy to peel	
	Winter squash: Includes butternut, acorn, and spaghetti squash

Winter Produce Spotlight: Onions

Onions are a staple vegetable and a member of the allium family, closely related to garlic, shallots, leeks, and chives. There are several varieties of onions, including yellow (or brown), red, and white onions, each with its own distinct flavor and best use in cooking. Additionally, there are sweet varieties, such as Vidalia and Walla Walla, which are less pungent and have a higher sugar content. Onions are generally divided into two categories based on the day length needed for bulb formation:

Short-day onions: These grow best in southern climates and are planted in the fall. They mature in late spring to early summer.

Long-day onions: These are grown in northern climates and are planted in early spring. They mature in late summer to early fall.

While onions are harvested at different times of the year depending on their type, they are available year-round due to their excellent storage capabilities.

Onions are also incredibly versatile in cooking and are used in various forms. Raw onions are used in salads, sandwiches, and as garnishes. Sautéing onions softens their texture and brings out their sweetness, while caramelizing them further enhances their natural sugars, adding depth to the flavor of soups, stews, and sauces. When roasted or grilled, onions develop a rich, sweet flavor, making them a great side dish or a component in various recipes. Roasting halved onions in water, white miso, and herbs produces an incredibly rich side dish that goes well with almost everything.

Pickling onions add a bright, tangy element to dishes and are often used as a condiment.

CARAMELIZED ONION AND MUSHROOM ON BUTTER BEAN MASH WITH PARSLEY

FOR THE BUTTER BEAN MASH

2 tablespoons olive oil (30 ml) or vegan butter (28 g)

2 garlic cloves, minced

2 cans (each 15 ounces [439 g]) butter beans, drained and rinsed

¼ cup (60 ml) unsweetened plant-based milk (such as almond or soy) or vegetable stock

Salt and pepper, to taste

A handful of fresh parsley, chopped

FOR THE CARAMELIZED ONIONS AND MUSHROOMS

Olive oil, for cooking

2 large onions, thinly sliced

2 cups (388 g) mushrooms (such as cremini or portobello), sliced

2 tablespoons (30 ml) balsamic vinegar

1 tablespoon (15 g) brown sugar (or maple syrup)

Salt and pepper, to taste

/

Yield: 4 portions

Butter beans are incredibly versatile, and they can be used in soups, stews, curries, and mash. Creating the mash out of beans boosts the protein content, while keeping the consistency creamy. Topped with caramelized onions for an added sweetness, mushrooms for texture and umami, and parsley for a fresh touch.

MAKE THE BUTTER BEAN MASH

In a pan, heat the olive oil or vegan butter over medium heat. Add garlic and cook until fragrant, about 1 minute. Add the butter beans and plant-based milk. Cook while mashing the beans with a fork or potato masher until they reach a creamy consistency. If needed, add more milk to adjust the texture. Season with salt and pepper and stir in half the chopped parsley. Keep warm.

MAKE THE CARAMELIZED ONIONS AND MUSHROOMS

In a separate pan, heat some olive oil over medium heat. Add the onions and cook, stirring occasionally, until they start to soften and become translucent. Add a pinch of salt and continue cooking the onions, stirring occasionally, until they turn golden brown and caramelize. This may take around 15 to 20 minutes. Add the mushrooms to the onions and cook until the mushrooms are tender and browned. Stir in the balsamic vinegar and brown sugar or maple syrup. Cook for another 2 to 3 minutes until the mixture is sticky and glazed. Season with salt and pepper to taste.

Spoon the butter bean mash onto serving plates. Top with the caramelized onion and mushroom mixture. Garnish with the remaining chopped parsley. Serve warm as a delightful main course or a hearty side dish.

For a little extra, this could be served with additional vegetables or a slice of fresh sourdough bread.

MUSHROOM AND LENTIL LASAGNA

FOR THE RED SAUCE

1 brown onion, diced

2 celery stalks, diced

4 garlic cloves, minced

1 large carrot or
2 medium-size, diced

1 cup (400 g) chestnut
mushrooms

1⅓ cups (150 g) walnuts,
divided

1 cup (237 ml) red wine

2 cups (100 g) sun-dried
tomatoes, roughly
chopped

1 tablespoon (16 g)
tomato paste

1 tablespoon (16 g)
white miso paste

1 tablespoon (15 ml)
soy sauce

1 tablespoon (15 ml)
balsamic vinegar

1 tablespoon (3 g)
dried oregano

¾ cup (200 g) puy lentils,
cooked

2 tins cherry tomatoes
(though you can use your
preferred tomato type),
chopped

Lentils are small, lens-shaped legumes that come in a variety of colors, including brown, green, red, and black. They are highly nutritious and packed with protein, fiber, and essential nutrients, making them a staple in many diets around the world. They do not require presoaking like many other legumes, which makes them a convenient choice for quick meals.

Lentils are used especially in vegetarian and vegan diets as a meat substitute due to their high protein content. Lentils are incredibly versatile in the kitchen. They are commonly used in soups and stews, thickening the broth and providing a hearty and comforting texture. They can also be added to salads for extra protein and fiber, and they pair well with a variety of vegetables and dressings. Lentils also are commonly mashed and used to make vegetarian burgers or meatballs. They have a texture that, when cooked, can mimic ground meat, especially when seasoned well, which makes them ideal for this delicious vegan lasagna.

MAKE THE RED SAUCE

Heat 2 tablespoons (30 ml) of olive oil from the jar of sun-dried tomatoes in a heavy-bottomed pan on medium-high heat. Once the oil is shimmering, add the onion. Cook for 8 to 10 minutes or until translucent. Next, add the celery, garlic, and carrot, sautéing for 10 minutes. Add the mushrooms and ¾ cup (100 g) of walnuts to a food processor and pulse until they resemble mince. Then add to the pot and sauté until the mushrooms start to release their juices. Once the liquid has evaporated, add in the red wine and simmer for 2 to 3 minutes. Add the sun-dried tomatoes, tomato paste, miso paste, soy sauce, balsamic vinegar, and oregano and stir to combine. Add in the lentils and cherry tomatoes and stir. Place the lid on the pot and simmer for 1 hour.

FOR THE WHITE SAUCE

½ cup (112 g) butter
(I used vegan; you can
also use ½ cup [118 ml]
olive oil instead)

1¼ cups (100 g)
plain flour

4¼ cups (1 L)
soy milk (or preferred
plant-based milk)

2 tablespoons (22 g)
nutritional yeast
(optional)

Handful of vegan cheese
(optional)

Lasagna sheets,
approximately
10–12 depending
on dish size

Cheese for topping

/

Yield: 8 portions

MAKE THE WHITE SAUCE

In the meantime, make the vegan bechamel sauce. Add the butter to a sauce-pan and let it melt. Once melted, add the flour, stirring to form a rue. Pour the soy milk into the pan a little at a time, stirring constantly. This helps to prevent your sauce from getting lumpy. It takes a little while, but it's worth it. If you would like to add a "cheesy" element to the bechamel sauce, add the yeast in now. Stir the sauce until the yeast is well incorporated. Once your sauce reaches a consistency that you're happy with, set it aside.

Preheat the oven to 375°F (190°C). Begin layering your lasagna in a large oven-proof dish. Start with a thin layer of the tomato sauce, a few walnuts, the white sauce, and then your lasagna sheets. Repeat until you either have no sauce left or have filled the dish. After your last layer of lasagna sheets, add the remaining white sauce and top with vegan cheese. Place in the oven and bake for 50 minutes covered, then 15 minutes uncovered. The cheese should have browned and the lasagna should be bubbling at the sides. Remove from the oven and allow to cool for 15 minutes before serving.

 NOTE

When meal prepping, I like to allow the lasagna to cool completely, split it into portions, and freeze.

FOR THE FILLING

1 cup (200 g) green or brown lentils (dried)

Olive oil, for cooking

1 large brown onion, chopped

2 cups (250 g) chestnut mushrooms, roughly chopped

2 garlic cloves, minced

1 can (14 ounces [396 g]) diced tomatoes

8 sun-dried tomatoes, roughly chopped

2 tablespoons (32 g) tomato paste

1 teaspoon dried thyme

1 teaspoon dried rosemary

½ teaspoon smoked paprika

Salt and pepper, to taste

2 cups (473 ml) vegetable broth or water

1 cup (135 g) frozen peas or mixed vegetables (optional)

FOR THE MASHED POTATO TOPPING

4 large potatoes, peeled and cubed

¼ cup (60 ml) unsweetened plant-based milk (such as almond or soy milk)

1 teaspoon Dijon mustard

2 tablespoons vegan butter (28 g) or olive oil (30 ml)

Salt and pepper, to taste

2 tablespoons (22 g) nutritional yeast (for a cheesy flavor) (optional)

/

Yield: 4 to 6 portions

STORE CUPBOARD SHEPHERD'S PIE

Creating a store cupboard shepherd's pie is a fantastic way to use pantry staples to make a hearty and comforting meal.

MAKE THE FILLING

Rinse the lentils and check for any debris. Set aside. In a large pan, heat the olive oil over medium heat. Add the onion, mushrooms, and garlic, cooking until the onions are translucent. Stir in the rinsed lentils, tomatoes, sun-dried tomatoes, tomato paste, thyme, rosemary, smoked paprika, salt, and pepper. Cook for a couple of minutes. Add the vegetable broth or water. Bring to a boil and then reduce to a simmer. Cover and cook for about 30 minutes, or until the lentils are tender. If you have frozen peas or mixed vegetables, add them in the last 5 minutes of cooking.

MAKE THE MASHED POTATO TOPPING

While the lentils are cooking, boil the potatoes in salted water until tender, about 15 to 20 minutes. Drain the potatoes and return them to the pot. Add the milk, mustard, and butter or olive oil and mash until smooth. Season with salt and pepper to taste. Stir in nutritional yeast if using.

Preheat the oven to 375°F (190°C). In a baking dish, spread the lentil mixture evenly. Top with the mashed potatoes, spreading evenly. You can use a fork to create ridges on top for a crispy texture. Place the dish in the oven and bake for about 20 minutes, or until the top is golden brown and the edges are bubbling. Allow the shepherd's pie to cool for a few minutes before serving.

The Conscious Kitchen

NUT ROAST WITH CRANBERRIES AND WALNUTS

FOR THE NUT ROAST

2 tablespoons (24 g) ground flaxseed (flax eggs)

Olive oil, for cooking

1 large brown onion, finely chopped

2 garlic cloves, minced

1 carrot, grated

1 celery stalk, finely chopped

1 cup (194 g) mushrooms, chopped

1 cup (85 g) chestnuts, cooked and peeled

2 cups (100 g) fresh cranberries, divided

1 cup (112 g) walnuts, roughly chopped

1 cup (256 g) almonds, roughly chopped

1 cup (120 g) breadcrumbs (use gluten-free if needed)

2 tablespoons (30 ml) soy sauce or tamari (gluten-free if needed)

1 teaspoon dried thyme

1 teaspoon dried rosemary

1 teaspoon smoked paprika

Salt and pepper, to taste

For me a nut roast isn't just enjoyed during the Christmas holidays. It has replaced the traditional Sunday lunch that I've often had with family after a long walk on a Sunday afternoon. The best thing about a nut roast is that it is so adaptable. You can change up the nuts, herbs, and accompaniments to suit your tastes. There will be lots of notes at the end of this recipe.

MAKE THE NUT ROAST

In a small bowl, mix the ground flaxseed with 6 tablespoons (89 ml) of water and set aside to thicken for about 15 minutes. Heat the olive oil in a large pan over medium heat. Add the onion and garlic, cooking until softened. Add the carrots, celery, and mushrooms. Cook until the vegetables are tender and the moisture from the mushrooms has evaporated. Stir in the chestnuts and 1 cup (50 g) of the fresh cranberries, cooking for another 2 to 3 minutes. Set aside to cool slightly.

In a large bowl, combine the walnuts, almonds, cooked vegetable mixture, breadcrumbs, flax eggs, soy sauce or tamari, thyme, rosemary, smoked paprika, salt, and pepper. Mix well until everything is evenly combined. Preheat the oven to 350°F (175°C). Line a loaf pan with parchment paper, allowing some overhang for easy removal later.

Cont. →

FOR THE GLAZE

2 tablespoons (30 ml) maple syrup

1 tablespoon (15 ml) balsamic vinegar

1 tablespoon (15 ml) olive oil

1 teaspoon Dijon mustard

/

Yield: 6 portions

MAKE THE GLAZE

Combine the ingredients for the glaze in a small bowl. Add the other cup of fresh cranberries into the loaf pan and pour over the glaze.

Then add the nut roast mixture on top and firmly press the mixture into the pan. Bake for 45 to 50 minutes, or until the nut roast is firm and the top is golden. Allow the nut roast to cool in the pan for about 10 to 15 minutes, then use the parchment paper to lift it out. Slice and serve warm.

NOTE

I like to serve this with a mushroom gravy, roasted potatoes, braised red cabbage, and roasted Brussel sprouts, but you can serve it with anything you like or have on hand. Now, by nature, a nut roast is incredibly versatile. You can make it like I have above, or you can make it like a baked risotto or without nuts at all and turn it into a lentil loaf. Everything can be substituted or amended to suit your tastes and what you have available in your pantry or budget.

BAKED SWEET POTATO, CHICKPEA SALAD, AND TAHINI DRESSING

This hearty dish combines the natural sweetness of baked sweet potatoes with the crispy, spiced chickpeas for a delightful contrast in textures. The freshness of the green salad complements the richness, while a creamy tahini dressing brings all the elements together with its nutty, smooth flavor. Perfect for a nutritious dinner or a fulfilling lunch.

FOR THE BAKED SWEET POTATOES

4 medium-size sweet potatoes, washed and pierced with a fork

FOR THE SPICED AND ROASTED CHICKPEAS

1 can (15 ounces [425 g]) chickpeas, drained, rinsed, and dried

1 tablespoon (15 ml) olive oil

1 teaspoon ground cumin

1 teaspoon smoked paprika

½ teaspoon garlic powder

Salt and pepper, to taste

FOR THE LEMON TAHINI DRESSING

¼ cup (64 g) tahini (sesame seed paste)

3 tablespoons (44 ml) lemon juice

1 garlic clove, minced

Salt and pepper, to taste

2–3 tablespoons (30–44 ml) ice water

FOR THE GREEN SALAD

2 cups (60 g) spinach, roughly chopped

1 cup (28 g) young Swiss chard leaves

1 cup (20 g) arugula

Drizzle of olive oil

Pinch of salt

FOR THE OPTIONAL GARNISHES

Fresh parsley, chopped

Red pepper flakes

A sprinkle of sesame seeds

/

Yield: 4 portions

MAKE THE BAKED SWEET POTATOES
Preheat the oven to 400°F (200°C). Place the sweet potatoes on a baking sheet and bake for 45 to 60 minutes, or until tender when pierced with a fork.

MAKE THE SPICED AND ROASTED CHICKPEAS
In a bowl, toss the chickpeas with olive oil, cumin, smoked paprika, garlic powder, salt, and pepper. Spread the chickpeas on a baking sheet lined with parchment paper. Roast in the oven (alongside the sweet potatoes) for about 20 to 30 minutes, stirring occasionally, until crispy and golden.

MAKE THE LEMON TAHINI DRESSING
In a small bowl, whisk together the tahini, lemon juice, garlic, salt, and pepper. Gradually add water to thin the dressing until it reaches your desired consistency.

MAKE THE GREEN SALAD
Combine the salad ingredients.

Once the sweet potatoes are done, let them cool slightly, then split them open lengthwise. Fluff the insides with a fork. Top each sweet potato with a generous amount of roasted chickpeas. Add your green salad. Drizzle the lemon tahini dressing over the sweet potatoes, chickpeas, and salad leaves. Garnish with chopped parsley, red pepper flakes, and sesame seeds, if desired.

Winter Produce Spotlight: Potatoes

Potatoes are tuberous root vegetables that belong to the *Solanaceae*, or nightshade, family, which also includes tomatoes, peppers, and eggplants. Originally from the Andes in South America, potatoes are now grown and consumed worldwide, making them a staple food in many cultures.

There are numerous varieties of potatoes, broadly categorized into starchy, waxy, and all-purpose.

Starchy potatoes: Including russet or Idaho, these have a high starch content and a fluffy texture when cooked. They're ideal for baking, mashing, and frying.

Waxy potatoes: Including red bliss or fingerling, these potatoes have a lower starch content and hold their shape well after cooking. They're great for boiling, roasting, and salads.

All-purpose potatoes: Including Yukon gold, these offer a balance between starchy and waxy, making them versatile for various cooking methods.

Potatoes are generally considered a cool-season crop. In terms of seasonality, spring-planted potatoes are harvested in late summer and fall, whereas in warmer climates potatoes can be planted in the fall for a late-winter or early-spring harvest. Although potatoes are harvested seasonally, they store well and are available year-round in stores. A few simple ways to prepare potatoes include boiling or steaming, baking or roasting, frying, mashing, adding to soups or stews, and pureeing to thicken dishes.

Winter Produce Spotlight: Beans

Beans are a type of legume, a family of plants that includes lentils, peas, and peanuts. They grow in pods and are valued for their high protein content and nutritional benefits, making them a staple in vegetarian and vegan diets. Some common types of beans include black beans, kidney beans, pinto beans, navy beans, garbanzo beans (chickpeas), and lima beans (butter bean). Each type of bean has its own distinct taste and texture, making them extra versatile in cooking.

Beans grow in a variety of climates and conditions, but they generally prefer warm temperatures and are typically grown in two forms:

Bush beans: These grow on short, bushy plants and don't require support. They tend to mature all at once, making them suitable for commercial harvesting.

Pole beans: These grow on long vines and need support, such as trellises or poles. They mature over a longer period and are often used in home gardens. Not only are they wonderful producers, but they're also beautiful vining plants that flower in all manner of colors, providing shade to other plants that need less sun.

Beans can be harvested in two stages: Green beans are the immature pods of the bean plant, harvested before the beans inside fully develop. It takes about 50 days for most varieties to mature enough to pick them, with new beans following regularly. You can expect to harvest from midsummer until early autumn They are eaten whole, pod and all, whereas dry beans are fully mature beans that are harvested when the pods have dried on the plant. This occurs at the end of the growing season, when the plant begins to die—though pods that are not harvested will eventually bulge, produce beans, and dry throughout the season. They are shelled and then the beans are used in a dried form, requiring soaking and cooking before consumption.

Beans are a nutritional powerhouse, providing a rich source of protein, fiber, vitamins, and minerals while also being low in fat. They are particularly important in plant-based diets as a major protein source. Their ability to absorb flavors makes them a favorite ingredient in many savory dishes worldwide, and their versatility to be pureed, mashed, or eaten whole adds to their popularity.

CHUNKY VEGETABLE, BUTTER BEAN, AND PASTA SOUP WITH SOURDOUGH FOCACCIA

2 tablespoons (30 ml) olive oil

1 large onion, diced

2 garlic cloves, minced

2 carrots, diced

2 celery stalks, diced

1 can (15 ounces [439 g]) butter beans, drained and rinsed

1 can (14 ounces [396 g]) diced tomatoes

6 cups (1.4 L) vegetable broth (I like roasted garlic for this recipe)

1 teaspoon dried oregano

1 teaspoon dried basil

Salt and pepper, to taste

1 cup (95 g) small pasta (such as shells, macaroni, or ditalini)

Fresh parsley, chopped (optional)

Vegan Parmesan cheese (optional)

Red pepper flakes (optional)

/

Yield: 4 to 6 portions

This soup, accompanied by an easy sourdough focaccia, is a straightforward and filling meal. It combines the heartiness of vegetables and butter beans with the comfort of pasta in a rich broth. The soup is paired perfectly with crusty sourdough focaccia for dipping and is designed for ease and convenience, making it ideal for a cozy evening meal or a comforting lunch.

Heat the olive oil in a large pot over medium heat. Add the onion and garlic, sautéing until the onion is translucent. Add the carrots and celery, cooking for another 5 minutes until they start to soften. Mix in the butter beans and tomatoes, including their juice. Add the vegetable broth to the pot. Bring the mixture to a boil.

Add the dried oregano, dried basil, salt, and pepper. Stir well. Once the soup is boiling, add the pasta. Reduce the heat to a simmer. Cook the soup for about 10 to 12 minutes, or until the pasta is al dente. Taste the soup and adjust the seasoning as needed. Let the soup simmer for a couple more minutes. Ladle the soup into bowls.

Garnish with chopped fresh parsley, vegan Parmesan cheese, and red pepper flakes, if desired. Serve the soup hot.

Cont. →

2 cups (473 ml) water

⅓ cup (100 g) sourdough starter

1½ teaspoons salt

4 cups (548 g) bread flour

2½ teaspoons dried rosemary

Olive oil

/

Yield: 1 loaf

SOURDOUGH FOCACCIA

Add the water to a large mixing bowl. Add the starter, and if it floats, it's ready. Roughly mix the starter into the water. Add the salt and mix. Then add the flour and rosemary. Mix to combine all the ingredients. Cover and set aside to rise for 30 minutes.

Do one set of stretches and folds. Add a little olive oil to the top, cover, and allow to double in size. Once your dough has doubled, pull the dough up and coil it in on itself. Place in a lined pan with a small drizzle of olive oil at the bottom. Allow the dough to rise until it fills the pan. Preheat the oven to 425ºF (218ºC). Drizzle more olive oil onto the surface of the dough, use your fingers to create dimples, and sprinkle over some flaky salt. Bake in the oven for 30 minutes. Check to see if it's done by assessing the color. If it is a nice golden brown, then it's ready.

Remove the focaccia from the oven and place on a cooling rack. Allow to cool for at least 40 minutes before serving.

NOTE

Focaccia is incredibly versatile and can be topped with almost anything your heart desires.

The Hungry Gap

The "hungry gap" is a term used primarily in the context of British agriculture and gardening. It refers to a period in late spring when the winter crops have been harvested and eaten, but the new season's crops are not yet ready to harvest. This gap typically occurs from April to early June in the UK and varies in the US due to its expansive size. Historically, this period was significant because food stores from the previous autumn would be dwindling or exhausted, and fresh produce was scarce. This made it a challenging time for people relying on their own gardens or local produce.

The exact timing and impact of the hungry gap can vary by region and year to year, depending on the climate and weather conditions. In the modern global food system, the impact of the hungry gap is less pronounced, as supermarkets and stores import produce from around the world. However, for those who focus on eating locally and seasonally, it can still be a time of limited variety. The end of winter means the last of the root vegetables and stored crops, such as potatoes, onions, and winter squashes, are typically used up. Many of the spring crops, such as early salads, peas, and new potatoes, are not yet ready to harvest during this period.

This is very much a time of waiting, and although it may appear a little bleak, it's the last phase before beauty and variety storm back into view with the new shoots and blossoms of spring. At this time, many rely heavily on foods they have preserved from the past summer, such as canned tomatoes, fermented cabbage, and pickled vegetables. This time is certainly one of reflection and anticipation. It's helpful to take stock of what you have left in your pantry, what was eaten quickly, and what you're most looking forward to. Each year provides a new experience to learn from and adapt the following year's plan.

What's in Season during the Hungry Gap?

Depending on the region, a few different things are possibly in season during this period. For example, in the UK you may find dandelion leaves, cabbage, carrots, kale, onions, potatoes, spring onions, watercress, wild garlic, and winter leaves in season. The appearance of wild garlic is the highlight of this period for me. You're most likely able to find this in the UK, and it can be found only by foraging. Wild garlic is abundant in wooded areas that are quite damp and can be used to make pesto, be added to your winter sauerkraut, or be baked into bread. Foraging is a huge part of seasonal eating in the UK, and people are careful to take only what they need—leaving the majority of the plant to allow it to come back year after year.

Strategies to Bridge the Gap

Gardeners and farmers use various strategies to bridge the hungry gap. These include planting early varieties of certain crops, using greenhouses or polytunnels to extend the growing season, and preserving food from previous seasons. Some hardy greens, such as kale and chard, can persist into the hungry gap, providing some fresh produce options.

Understanding and acknowledging the hungry gap is part of a broader movement toward sustainable and mindful eating, where people are more in tune with the natural growing cycles and the limitations of their local agricultural systems. In many regions across the world, there will be a similar "gap" when seeds are sown and all that is left to do is wait. During these times, we can make use of microgreens and sprouts, a cheap, compact, and extremely fast way to provide fresh nutrients throughout the winter and hungry gap months. It is also possible to make use of small growing systems that utilize water rather than soil. These can be small and compact or rather large and sturdy, and capable of growing a large array of fresh foods.

How to Grow Microgreens and Sprouts

Sprouts are very easy to grow and only take around 7 days to mature. You'll need a glass jar and a lid that allows water to pass through but not the seeds. Add 1 to 2 tablespoons (3–6 g) of sprout seeds to a glass jar. These include broccoli, radish, kale, alfalfa, and many more. Cover with water and allow to soak for 24 hours, then drain. Each morning, rinse your seeds to keep them moist, draining the remaining water afterward. Keep your jar completely upturned or at an angle so the water can drain. After 2 days you should see some sprouting, and after 5 to 7 days, your sprouts should be ready to eat. Remove from the jar and place the sprouts in an airtight container and put in the fridge. Eat within 3 to 5 days. Clean your jar and lid thoroughly before starting the process again.

Unlike sprouts, microgreens need soil to grow. Place around 2 inches (5 cm) of soil in a shallow tray and generously sprinkle your microgreen seeds over the top. Gently cover with a layer of soil and then water. Water your microgreens every day with a light shower. Microgreens are ready to harvest between 8 and 21 days. Cut at least ⅓ inch (1 cm) above the soil and you should be able to harvest again in another couple of weeks. My favorite microgreens to grow are green peas, cilantro, basil, and wheatgrass. The possibilities are endless though.

REDUCING FOOD WASTE: COOK WITH IT

When the food we don't eat ends up in the garbage, it's hard to conceptualize how much food we're actually wasting. Why is this a problem? With no oversight or data, we simply can't keep track of our impact, and the consequences compound and become quite devastating. Landfills aren't aerated properly for true decomposition to take place, so organic matter cannot return to the earth. This unfortunately means that the food that ends up in our bins could be contributing to climate change. This may sound pretty dramatic, but there are plenty of ways for us to combat this growing problem.

In the next two chapters, I'll share with you my two-pronged approach to reducing food waste. The first method is to examine meal planning and, specifically, how to use up veggie scraps, cook down peels, and reuse them in other cooking and household projects. Then with the waste you simply cannot eat or repurpose, we'll go through methods for composting and how you can take your composting skills to the garden to complete the food cycle. Reducing food waste and learning to compost efficiently are fundamental pillars of keeping a conscious kitchen.

First, let's look at ways to use food up before it becomes waste.

Manage Meal Plans

The tool I most rely on to reduce food waste is meal planning. All you need to plan out a few meals and write a grocery list is about 20 minutes each week. A little planning can reduce impulse buying, buying too much, and neglecting those last few veggies in the back of your fridge.

Before planning out my meals, I'll do a pantry sweep and look at what's left in the fridge. From there, I can decide what meals I need or want to make this week based off the ingredients I have available to me. If I have a couple of cans of cannellini beans leftover and a bunch of kale in the fridge, for example, maybe I'll make a soup. Or if I'm at a loss when it comes to ideas, I'll search "meal ideas for cannellini beans" online. It seems rudimentary, but without a reminder I will often forget that searching for meal ideas based on a single ingredient is possible. It's hard to predict what kind of mood you'll be in throughout the week, and I know how important it is to eat intuitively. So, consider a varied week of meals with a couple of staples and your favorite snacks.

Sample Meal Plan One

Monday	Tuesday	Wednesday	Thursday	Friday	Saturday	Sunday
Breakfast: Creamy porridge with seasonal fruit, yogurt, and maple syrup	Breakfast: Overnight oats with berry compote and almond milk	Breakfast: Mushrooms on toast with sautéed spinach	Breakfast: Creamy porridge with seasonal fruit, yogurt, and maple syrup	Breakfast: Overnight oats with berry compote and almond milk	Brunch: Homemade waffles with fresh fruit, yogurt, and maple syrup	Breakfast: Breakfast burrito with tofu scramble, avocado, fresh salsa, and roasted potatoes
Lunch: Chickpea salad with salad greens on crusty bread	Lunch: Lentil salad with roasted vegetables, parsley, and lemon	Lunch: Leftover tortellini soup with crusty bread	Lunch: Sweet potato, butter bean, and roasted tomato soup topped with garlic croutons	Lunch: Panzanella using leftover bread and crispy chickpeas		Lunch: Homemade falafel bowl with beet hummus, couscous, pickles, and lettuce
Dinner: Red lentil curry with rice or naan	Dinner: Tortellini soup with chunky vegetables	Dinner: Fried rice with veggies that need eating and crispy tempeh with a soy dressing	Dinner: Sesame ginger sushi bowl with beet poké and edamame beans	Dinner: Peanut butter tofu rice bowl with fresh veggie slaw	Dinner: Creamy mushroom stroganoff	Dinner: Coconut curry noodle bowl
Snacks: Seasonal fruit, nuts	Snacks: Peanut butter and apple	Snacks: Toast with jam or hummus	Snacks: Fruit and nut bar	Snacks: Homemade muffin	Snacks: Energy balls or fruit	Snacks: Yogurt with fruit and granola

The Conscious Kitchen

Sample Weekly Meal Plans

Here are two examples of quite varied weeks of meals, including simple snacks, leftovers, and some ideas for using up stale bread and day-old rice. One thing I look for in my meal plan is the ease and ability to repeat meals. This reduces cooking and planning time, especially for busy people. I also consider a couple of meals that can be made ahead and stored in either the fridge or freezer for later in the week. If you don't like meal prep, try food prep instead. Food prep focuses on individual ingredients or elements that make the process of cooking easier, rather than

Sample Meal Plan Two

Monday	Tuesday	Wednesday	Thursday	Friday	Saturday	Sunday
Breakfast: Chia pudding with coconut milk, berries, and nut butter	Breakfast: Homemade granola with mixed nuts, seasonal fruit, and plant milk	Breakfast: Smashed green peas on toast with lemon and salt (think avocado toast but higher protein)	Breakfast: Quick bagel with jam and peanut butter, or vegan carrot lox and cream cheese	Breakfast: Smoothie with seasonal fruit, almond milk, and vegan protein	Brunch: Cinnamon spiced carrot waffles (think carrot cake) with seasonal fruit	Breakfast: Mini English breakfast with mushrooms, hash browns, tofu scramble, and toast
Lunch: Noodle salad with fresh cilantro, peanut dressing, and shredded veggies	Lunch: Meal-prepped vegan quiche with salad	Lunch: Leek and watercress risotto topped with toasted nuts	Lunch: Meal-prepped vegan quiche and salad	Lunch: Spicy vegan dan dan noodles		Lunch: Caponata with couscous
Dinner: Basil pesto with toasted seeds and red lentil pasta	Dinner: Pulled king oyster mushroom, peanut, and chili noodles	Dinner: Sticky miso eggplant with shaved broccoli and rice	Dinner: Black bean chili soup with corn dumpling	Dinner: Lasagna with greens on the side	Dinner: Veggie sausage casserole with apples and cider	Dinner: Tahini and "honey"-roasted cauliflower with jeweled pilau rice
Snacks: Seasonal fruit, nuts	Snacks: Everything bagel or chopped veggies with hummus	Snacks: Toast with jam or hummus	Snacks: Apple with crunchy peanut butter	Snacks: Oatmeal breakfast cookies	Snacks: Smoothie with seasonal fruit, almond milk, and vegan protein	Snacks: Yogurt with fruit and granola

preparing the entire meal in advance. An example of this may be preparing a Thai green curry paste in advance or chopping and storing vegetables so that they're ready to go. This is especially helpful for meals such as salads that can be assembled rather than cooked. Other examples of food prep include roasting a sheet pan of seasoned vegetables, preparing two different salad dressings, and making a bowl of couscous with veggie stock. These all can be stored separately and tossed together in any combination. This method also allows for flexibility if you have an extra cucumber or tomato that needs eating up.

For these meal plans, I have purposely included leftovers or meal prepped for one or two of the lunches, because this is probably our most time-restricted meal. This is handy for commuters as it's ready to go in the morning without much thought, and lunch is essentially planned the night before. I have also included words like "seasonal," to encourage you to opt for foods that are likely locally grown. Aside from a big part of creating a conscious kitchen, eating seasonally also gives us foods to look forward to. Much like the feeling of dragging your summer clothes out from under your bed for the season, tasting the first strawberry or tomato of the year feels exceptionally special.

Manage Grocery Lists

Okay, so you've done your pantry sweep, you've looked through the fridge, and you've made your meal plan for the week. Next, you'll want to write your grocery list. We discussed in chapter 1 how to shop and where to get your groceries (see page 18), so we won't go into much detail here. However, if you need a little extra help sticking to your list, here are a few tactics I've learned over the years.

1. Don't go shopping when you're hungry; you're far more likely to pick up items you don't want and aren't on your list.

2. If possible, go to the store when it's slightly quieter so you do not feel rushed. This tends to be during off-peak hours, such as in late morning or early afternoon. However, this is not possible for everyone.

If I'm having a particularly taxing week, I'll refer back to my little book of recipes for ideas. This is one of my favorite ways to keep track of the recipes I frequently make. It's a very simple list of meals with their corresponding ingredients list. I usually keep this book among my shopping bags, so if I forget or simply don't have time to write a meal plan, I already have a backup to help me stay on track. You can take this one step further and save all the recipes you create or find in a document and pull them together into either a digital or hard-copy book of recipes. I like my handwritten book of ingredients, but my husband has digital folders all neatly labeled and organized into breakfast, lunch, and dinners. So, find what organization system works for you and make sure to keep it handy or easily accessible.

Learning how to pair flavors is a really helpful skill. It enables you to swap out ingredients and alter recipes to favor what you have. For example, if a recipe calls for broccoli, but you have only spinach or cauliflower, knowing a comparable flavor helps you make an interesting or effective substitute. This skill has informed a lot of my decisions when trying to veganize old favorites too. Mushrooms, miso, and coffee have enabled me to achieve a rich umami flavor despite eliminating the meat element. In this way, it can be yet another tool in your kit to reduce food waste in the home.

Eat the Whole Vegetable

Exploring the whole vegetable also can be a learning curve for those used to throwing out cauliflower leaves, discarding the green bits on spring onions, and composting broccoli stalks. There are, of course, inventive ways to use these bits up, but, put simply, these bits pack a punch. The green part of the onion is often used raw and sprinkled on top of dishes, whereas the white part is mostly fried with other aromatics. To some, this may seem incredibly simple, but I never knew the green part was edible—so I assume some other people won't too. Here are some specifics for using up the whole vegetable:

1. Add broccoli stalks to veggie broth, chop up thinly and add to stir-fries, or make them into fries.

2. Slice cauliflower leaves very thinly and add them into curry, slaw, and salad recipes as an extra green.

3. Onion skins can be made into homemade onion powder, and the same can be done with garlic skins. See the recipe in the next section (see page 145).

4. Carrot greens can be blended into any pesto.

5. Thick kale stalks can be thinly shredded and eaten or added to veggie broth to enhance the flavor.

6. Potato skins can be either left on or tossed with olive oil, salt, and pepper and baked in the oven to make a crispy topping or snack.

7. Stale bread can be made into croutons, added to a panzanella, or blended into breadcrumbs and kept in the freezer.

Food Waste Recipes

Despite our best efforts to use the whole food, there will always be leftovers or bits of things we have no idea what to do with. So, I've come up with some inventive ways to use up peels and ends, repurpose leftover rice, and make fermented goods from waste. Honestly, however, the easiest thing will always be to chop it up really small and throw it in whatever you're making. You don't need to overcomplicate it, especially if you're just looking for simple ways to keep a conscious kitchen.

LEFTOVER FRIED RICE

FOR THE SAUCE

3 garlic cloves, minced

½-inch (1 cm) piece fresh ginger, minced

2 tablespoons (30 ml) soy sauce

1½ teaspoons (7 ml) dark soy sauce

1 tablespoon (15 ml) chili oil (optional)

1½ teaspoons (7 ml) rice wine vinegar

2 tablespoons (30 ml) maple syrup, or sweetener of choice

1 teaspoon onion powder

FOR THE LEFTOVER FRIED RICE

Vegetables of choice

2 cups (450 g) leftover rice

Sesame seeds, sliced spring onions, and chopped cilantro (optional)

/

Yield: ½-cup (118 ml) jar

Leftover rice is perfect for making fried rice. It also pairs well with veggies, herbs, and that quarter onion that's been sitting in the fridge. Fried rice is great for busy people because it really can be a "chop it up, throw it in"–type meal. The most important thing is to have a "go to" sauce that can be poured in to add flavor and lots of umami. Here is my favorite combination.

MAKE THE SAUCE

Add the garlic and ginger to a bowl. Add the rest of the sauce ingredients and mix thoroughly. You can also substitute the chili oil for peanut butter if you'd like a nuttier sauce. If you do this, make sure to add ice cold water, 1 tablespoon (15 ml) at a time, until you reach a pourable consistency.

MAKE THE LEFTOVER FRIED RICE

Cook the vegetables, add your rice, and stir to warm.

Then add in your sauce and coat everything evenly. You can top with sesame seeds, spring onions, and cilantro.

 NOTE

This sauce also can be used as a marinade for tofu. Simply follow the same method and add to a reusable bag or dish. Add your pressed tofu and coat thoroughly. Once your tofu is coated, pop in the fridge and marinate for 2 to 8 hours.

INAUTHENTIC ARANCINI

The best thing about this recipe is that it can be altered to suit your preferences and whatever you have lying around. You can keep it simple and just use leftover rice and kimchi. Or pack it full of flavor by mixing the shiitake mushrooms, carrot, spring onion, and a soy dressing. This is a fun one to experiment with, so don't limit yourself and get creative.

FOR THE RICE BALLS

1 carrot, diced

3 shiitake mushrooms, rehydrated and chopped

1 tablespoon (1 g) fresh cilantro, chopped

1 cup (225 g) leftover rice

1 teaspoon garlic powder

1 teaspoon onion powder

1 tablespoon (15 ml) soy sauce

1 tablespoon (8 g) sesame seeds

½ teaspoon sesame oil

FOR THE COATING

3 tablespoons (24 g) flour

1 tablespoon (15 ml) plant milk (you may need a little extra to get the consistency right)

3 tablespoons (21 g) breadcrumbs

Avocado oil, or any high-temperature oil

/

Yield: 2 portions

MAKE THE RICE BALLS

Add the carrots, shiitake mushrooms, and fresh cilantro to a mixing bowl. Add the leftover rice, garlic powder, and onion powder and fold gently to combine. Next add the soy sauce, sesame seeds, and sesame oil, and once again fold gently to combine.

MAKE THE COATING

Mix your flour and milk to form a thick batter. Set up two plates and put your breadcrumbs on one and the flour and milk mixture on the other.

Dip your hands in a small bowl of water and scoop up some of the rice mixture. Form into a ball in your hands. Next, coat the newly formed rice ball in the flour mixture, then in the breadcrumbs. Repeat until all the rice mixture is used up.

Heat a cast-iron pan, or any heavy-bottomed pan, and add ½ inch (1 cm) of high-temperature oil. When tiny bubbles start to appear, add your rice balls to the pan. Cook for 2 to 3 minutes on each side, or until they are golden brown. Transfer to a plate and eat immediately.

VEGETABLE PEEL BROTH

2 tablespoons vegan butter (28 g) or olive oil (30 ml)

4–5 cups (470–1,100 g) veggie scraps

1 large brown onion, roughly chopped

6 garlic cloves, roughly chopped

3 dried shiitake mushrooms

Fresh or dried thyme (optional)

10 peppercorns

2 teaspoons salt

1 tablespoon (16 g) miso paste (optional)

/

Yield: 8 cups (2 L)

Use your leftover veggie peels to make veggie broth. If you've been thinking about making your own veggie scrap broth for a while but need a little guidance, here is the recipe I created and swear by. There are a few extra ingredients, but they level up the flavor and are worth the effort. This recipe is also designed to be doubled, or tripled, depending on how many scraps you need to use up.

Add the butter or olive oil to a deep pot. Once hot, add the veggie scraps, onion, and garlic. Brown the veggies for 6 to 8 minutes. Once the vegetables have softened, add 8 cups (2 L) of water, the shiitake mushrooms, thyme (if using), and peppercorns and bring to a boil. Once boiling, reduce the heat and simmer for 1 to 2 hours. When your broth is almost ready, strain the liquid and add back to the pot. While simmering, add in the salt and miso paste, if using, and stir. At this point, you want to taste the broth and see if it needs a little more salt. If not, pour into jars and allow to cool. Place a lid on the jars and store in the fridge or freezer.

NOTE

If storing in the freezer, make sure you leave ¾ inch (2 cm) of space between the top of the liquid and the lid. If storing in the fridge, use within a week. Having homemade broth on hand is very helpful for quick meals such as soups, sauces, and curries.

ONION AND GARLIC POWDERS

Onion or onion skins
(or both)

Garlic skins

/

Yield: 1 small spice jar

I recently discovered that you can actually turn your onion and garlic skins into their own powders, and you'll never need to buy onion powder again. Homemade garlic powder saves waste, tastes better, and lasts a long time. And the best thing? It's incredibly simple to do.

Spread out your onion and garlic skins on a sheet and place in a dehydrator or in the oven at 135°F (57°C) for 8 to 10 hours or until fully dehydrated. Remove and allow to cool. Once cooled, place in a blender and blitz until the skins become a powder. Add the powder to a clean jar and place the lid on. This can be kept in the pantry for 3 months.

APPLE CIDER VINEGAR

6 cups (660 g) apple scraps, cores, peels, or pieces of apple

3 tablespoons (39 g) granulated sugar, though any will do

½ gallon (2.25 L) filtered water

EQUIPMENT

One ½ gallon (2.25 L) jar, wide mouth

One glass fermenting weight

Swing lid storage bottles for finished product

/

Yield: ½ gallon (2.25 L)

Once you start making apple cider vinegar at home, it's likely you'll never go back. It's incredibly cheap to make, tastes delicious, and utilizes scraps that would have otherwise gone to waste. Here is a straight-forward recipe that requires only a little time and patience.

After peeling and coring the apples, place the scraps into the glass jar. Fill approximately ¾ of the jar. Next add the sugar and filtered water. The water should fully cover the apple scraps. It's important to keep the contents fully submerged to prevent the growth of bad bacteria that could spoil your hard work. To do this, add your fermentation weight to the jar and lightly press down on the apples.

Cover the jar with a thin piece of cloth and secure it with a rubber band. Then place the jar somewhere cool and dark, such as a kitchen cupboard. Allow the apples to ferment and create the vinegar. This could take around 4 weeks, depending on the temperature of your house. The perfect temperature for fermenting is 70°F (21°C), so if your home is a little cooler, give the apple cider vinegar a little more time.

You should notice an alien-like disk forming on top of the vinegar. This is the mother and can be used in your next batch to speed up the process. It can also replace the need for sugar. It is similar to the symbiotic culture of bacteria and yeast (SCOBY) you would use to make kombucha. You can store the mother in your fridge with a little vinegar until you're ready to use it again.

Check the fermentation every couple of days to ensure the apples are still fully submerged and make any adjustments if need be. You always can top up the jar with filtered water if the apples are no longer submerged. Once you have created the vinegar, strain the apples so only the liquid is left. Place back in the jar and once again cover with a thin cloth. Allow to ferment for 2 to 3 more weeks. Taste the vinegar, and if you're happy with its flavor, decant into your swing bottles and store. If not, allow to ferment for another few days and keep tasting.

Compost your apple scraps after straining.

Leftover Citrus Peels

If your house is anything like mine, then citrus plays a major role in your everyday cooking. Whether it's adding lime juice to homemade guacamole, lemon to a tahini dressing, or orange to chocolate fudge brownies, there are always lots of skins leftover. You may have already heard of reusing your lemon peels to make a DIY surface cleaner, or just feeding them to the worms. But there are so many more ways that you can use citrus peels in your kitchen. Not only does citrus brighten dishes and add that tangy flavor we all love, but combined with sugar, citrus peels can be candied or even dried into powders.

CANDIED LEMON AND ORANGE PEELS

2 large oranges

2 lemons

2 cups (473 ml) water, plus more for blanching

2 cups (400 g) granulated sugar, plus extra for coating

/

Yield: 2 16-ounce (473 ml) jars

For me, candied peels are one of the most versatile ways to reuse peels, especially if you love baking. They make great treats that add a burst of citrus flavor and sweetness to a variety of dishes, from cakes and cookies to cocktails and salads.

Wash the oranges and lemons thoroughly. Cut the top and bottom off each fruit, and then score the skin into quarters. Carefully peel the fruit to remove the skin in large pieces, trying to keep the peel intact. Use a knife to scrape off as much of the bitter white pith from the inside of the peels as possible.

Cut the peels into strips about ¼ inch (6 mm) wide. Bring a large pot of water to a boil. Add the peel strips and boil for about 2 minutes. Drain the peels, then rinse them under cold water. Repeat this blanching process two more times with fresh water each time. This helps remove bitterness.

In the same pot, combine 2 cups (473 ml) of water and the granulated sugar. Stir over low heat until the sugar dissolves, then bring to a simmer. Add the blanched peel strips to the simmering syrup. Reduce the heat and simmer gently, uncovered, for about 45 minutes to 1 hour, or until the peels become translucent. Avoid stirring too often to prevent the peels from breaking. You can gently swirl the pot instead.

Carefully remove the peels from the syrup using a slotted spoon and lay them out on a wire rack over a baking sheet to catch drips. Allow the peels to dry for at least 4 to 6 hours or overnight. They should become slightly tacky but not wet.

Cont. ➜

Once the peels are dry, toss them in granulated sugar until they are well coated. Shake off any excess sugar. Place the sugared peels back on the wire rack to dry for another 1 to 2 hours.

Store the candied peels in an airtight container at room temperature. They can last for several weeks.

LEMON SALT

3 lemons

3 tablespoons (54 g) flaky salt, or any other coarse salt

/

Yield: 6 tablespoons (108 g)

Lemon salt is the mixture of lemon zest and sea salt—fairly straightforward but packs a punch. I prefer to use flaky salt and grind in a pestle and mortar, but you can use a bowl and spoon. You can play around with this recipe, substituting lemon peel for lime, grapefruit, or orange too.

Zest the lemons into a bowl and add the salt. If using a pestle and mortar, crush the mixture together. If using a bowl and spoon, mix together and use the back of the spoon to crush the zest and salt together. We're looking for a well-combined mixture that is fragrant and broken down. Store in an airtight container, in a cool, dry place, for up to 2 weeks. Reduce the quantities if you will not use the salt up in that time.

DIY LEMON OR LIME VINEGAR CLEANER

Peel of 2 whole lemons or 2 whole limes

8 cups (2 L) white distilled cleaning vinegar, 6 percent acidity

It's no secret that vinegar is an excellent cleaner, but people often complain about the smell it leaves behind. Though adding lemon will not completely remove the smell, it certainly lightens it. Making the DIY cleanser is simple.

Using a spoon, remove any remaining pulp from the inside of the lemon, making sure to really scrape down the inside. Slice into chunks that will fit inside your bottle of choice and pour over the vinegar. Replace the lid and allow it to sit on the counter for around 2 weeks or longer. When you're ready to use the infused vinegar, make sure to dilute it with 50 percent water. Add your 50/50 vinegar and water mix to a reusable bottle and use on most surfaces to disinfect, cut through grease, and clean.

Lemon as a Cleaning Agent

Lemon is an affordable and versatile cleaning agent, and when coupled with other ingredients, it can transform your kitchen and bathroom. You can use leftover lemons that have just been juiced as a scrubber of sorts. Gently squeezing and rubbing it over taps and the base of your sink will help to lift limescale or you can use it to decalcify your kettle. Fill your kettle with water and add in the lemon peels, boil, and allow to sit for 1 hour. Then rinse.

DIY CITRUS ESSENTIAL OILS

Citrus peels (oranges, lemons, limes, grapefruits, etc.)

Vodka (or any high-proof, neutral grain alcohol)

Water (optional, for dilution)

EQUIPMENT

Food processor

Glass jar with a tight-fitting lid

Strainer or cheesecloth

Small dark glass bottle for storage

A surprising way to reuse your citrus peels is to make essential oil with them. This method involves a simple extraction process that captures the fragrant citrus oils. This process does not produce pure essential oil, as that requires steam distillation. Therefore, this recipe has a shelf life of several weeks. Always do a patch test before using homemade oils on the skin to check for any allergic reactions, and do not ingest this oil. This DIY method is a fun and accessible way to create your own citrus-infused oil at home, perfect for use in homemade cleaning products.

Use the food processor to chop the citrus peels into smaller pieces, which will increase the surface area and help release more oils. Place the chopped citrus peels in the glass jar. Pour enough vodka over the peels to completely cover them. The alcohol acts as a solvent to extract the oils from the peels. Seal the jar tightly and shake gently to mix. Store the jar in a cool, dark place for about 1 to 2 weeks. Shake the jar once a day to help the extraction process.

After the infusion period, strain the mixture through a strainer or cheese-cloth into another container to remove the solid bits of peel. For a clearer oil, strain a second time or let the mixture sit undisturbed for a day and then decant the clearer top layer.

Transfer the strained liquid to a shallow dish and leave it in a well-ventilated area to allow the alcohol to evaporate naturally. This process might take a few days. The rate of evaporation will depend on the surface area of the liquid and the room temperature. Alternatively, you can gently heat the liquid in a water bath to speed up the evaporation, but be careful not to overheat and degrade the oils.

Once the alcohol has completely evaporated, you should be left with a concentrated citrus oil. Transfer the oil to a small, dark glass bottle for storage. Dark glass helps protect the oil from light, which can degrade it over time. Label the bottle with the type of citrus and the date.

CITRUS PEEL POTPOURRI

Citrus peels: from oranges, lemons, limes, grapefruits, etc.

Dried flowers: such as lavender, roses, or chamomile

Spices: whole cinnamon sticks, cloves, star anise, or cardamom pods

Essential oils (optional): a few drops of citrus, lavender, or any preferred essential oils

Dried herbs: rosemary, thyme, or mint

EQUIPMENT

Baking sheet

Parchment paper

Airtight container

Creating a homemade potpourri with citrus peels is another way to repurpose fruit peels and infuse your home with a fresh, natural fragrance. This DIY project is simple and allows for a lot of creativity in choosing ingredients that complement citrus. Here's a basic recipe to get you started, but feel free to customize it with your preferred scents and materials.

Preheat the oven to its lowest setting (around 200°F [90°C], if possible). Thinly slice the citrus peels or tear them into small pieces for quicker drying. Place the peels on a baking sheet lined with parchment paper in a single layer. Put the baking sheet in the oven, leaving the door slightly ajar to allow moisture to escape. Bake for 1 to 3 hours, or until the peels are completely dry but not burned. The time needed can vary based on oven temperature and peel thickness. Alternatively, you can air-dry the peels in a warm, dry place for several days.

Once the citrus peels are dried, mix them in a bowl with your chosen dried flowers, spices, and dried herbs. Gently toss the mixture to evenly distribute the ingredients. If desired, sprinkle a few drops of essential oil over the mixture to intensify the fragrance. Mix well to distribute the oil evenly.

Transfer the mixture to an airtight container. Seal the container and store it in a cool, dark place for a few weeks. Shake the container every few days to redistribute the scents.

After the curing period, place your potpourri in decorative bowls or sachets around your home. To refresh the scent over time, add more essential oils or replace some of the older ingredients.

CUSTOMIZATION TIPS

Feel free to experiment with different combinations of citrus peels, dried flowers, and spices to create a scent profile that you love. Seasonal variations can offer a refreshing change; consider adding pine cones and evergreen sprigs for a winter-themed potpourri, or dried apple slices and cinnamon for a cozy autumn vibe.

Of course, this isn't an exhaustive list of what you can do with vegetable peels, stalks, and other ends, so here are a few ideas or thought starters to get you into a creative headspace.

1. Make vegetable peel fritters or pakoras with spiced chickpeas.

2. Crisp potato peels to make chips.

3. Coat and fry broccoli stalks.

4. Thinly slice peels (such as potato, carrot, or beet peels), toss them with a little oil and your favorite seasonings, and bake until crispy.

5. Quick-pickle peels and ends, such as cucumber ends or carrot peels, in vinegar, water, and spices for a tangy snack.

6. Use thinly sliced or diced vegetable stalks and ends in stir-fries. Broccoli stalks, for example, are delicious when cooked this way.

7. Greens such as carrot tops and radish leaves can make a delicious pesto. Blend with nuts, cheese, garlic, and olive oil.

8. Use peels from vegetables such as onions and beets to create natural dyes for fabric or Easter eggs.

9. Add flavor to mushroom stock by including vegetable ends and peels during the simmering process.

10. Add cucumber or citrus peels to water for a refreshing drink.

11. Boil apple peels, cinnamon, and cloves to make a delicious homemade tea.

12. Potato peels can be boiled and blended into soups to naturally thicken them.

13. Some vegetable ends and greens can be frozen and added to smoothies for extra nutrients.

14. Use clean, broken eggshells and coffee grounds mixed with soil as a nutrient-rich potting mix for plants.

15. Some vegetable scraps (make sure they're safe for pets) can be a healthy treat for your pets.

I could probably write an entire book about how to reduce food waste in your home, so I encourage you to use this chapter as a starting point and continue to look for other ways to make the most of the food we buy. In this chapter, we've looked at ways to prevent food from becoming waste in the first place. This is strategy one. In the next chapter, we'll look at the food we simply cannot eat, what to do with it, and how to compost anywhere.

REDUCING FOOD WASTE: COMPOST AND REPLANT IT

In the area of sustainable living and responsible waste management, composting is arguably the best solution to food waste. Why? Because it transforms a waste product into something beneficial, both to our gardens and to the earth's soil health in general. It also prevents the harmful buildup of gases trapped in landfills, which directly contributes to climate change. It's estimated that, globally, we waste approximately 1.4 billion tons of food every year, with 40 million tons coming from the US alone. A proportion of this comes from the real or perceived food spoilage in our homes. So, if we were able to turn that waste into something useful, we could attempt to mitigate a small piece of that rotten pie.

Now, composting is not a one-size-fits-all endeavor; it is a dynamic and adaptable process that can be tailored to suit myriad circumstances. Whether you live in a small apartment in the city with limited space or in the countryside with access to a garden, there exists a composting solution perfectly attuned to your unique needs. This chapter serves as your guide through the diverse landscape of composting methods. We'll dive into the Bokashi method, the Hot Compost method, and vermicompost; touch on cold composting and resources offered by local composting services; and even provide a letter template to ask your local authority to install recycling services in your area.

Once we get a handle on composting, we'll discuss how to use it to start growing your own herbs and produce in your garden. My relationship with food changed when I started to grow my own—to feel the soil, place each seed, and watch the flowers slowly die and turn to fruit—and I hope yours will too. Keeping a garden granted me an understanding of the value we place on food, or lack thereof, and what it takes to produce one potato, blueberry, or green pea. Gardening doesn't have to be limited to those with acres of land to spare; you can start with some pots of basil growing on your windowsill. It's hard to truly fail when it comes to gardening—it's all a beautiful experiment that will produce something delicious in the end.

In this chapter, I hope to instill in you a sense of competence and excitement, while also eliciting a deep appreciation for how easily accessible food is to a lot of us. I hope by the end of this chapter you feel empowered to start composting and plant just a few seeds this year.

Vermicompost

I was very skeptical when I first heard about the idea of vermicompost (composting with worms). My friend Naomi had a box that sat on the top of her houseboat, full of worms that seemed to consume any amount of food waste she produced at an alarming rate. I thought it would be a messy solution and that it would likely smell very bad. Of course, I was wrong. These clever little worms are incredible composters and can be kept inside a small apartment, in a garden, or in a cozy corner of a garage. Since adding worms to my composting rota, I've become certain that they are an almost perfect solution for most homes. Here's everything you need to know about composting with worms and how they help maintain a conscious kitchen.

Vermicomposting is a natural and efficient process that transforms organic waste into nutrient-rich compost with the help of earthworms. This method harnesses the digestive efficiency of specific worm species, most commonly *Eisenia fetida*, known as red wigglers, or *Lumbricus rubellus*. These worms have an extraordinary ability to break down organic matter into a high-quality fertilizer through their feeding and digestion processes.

Vermicomposting can be done in various containers or specialized systems, meaning worm factories specifically designed to allow worms to travel upward to find the food source. A simple bin with adequate aeration and moisture control is often sufficient for small-scale home composting. You can even get rather aesthetically pleasing worm bins that can be unobtrusive in small apartments. Shredded newspaper, cardboard, or coconut coir serves as bedding material for the worms. This provides a comfortable environment and a carbon-rich base for the composting process. Every time you start a new tray, you layer in these materials, adding organic matter on top. Things such as rock dust are also helpful, as it helps the worms to digest the material.

Kitchen scraps such as fruit and vegetable peels, coffee grounds, and other nonmeat, nondairy organic materials are added to the bin regularly. It's important to avoid citrus, onions, and spicy foods that worms may find less palatable. Although I have found, in smaller doses, they will eat them. The worms consume the organic waste, breaking it down into simpler compounds through their digestive processes. This digestion produces nutrient-rich worm castings, also known as vermicompost.

After a few months, the vermicompost is ready for harvest. The "compost" or organic matter will be dark and moist, and there will be little-to-no obvious recognizable food items. Worms are typically separated from the compost, and the finished vermicompost can be used to enrich garden soil, potting mixes, or as a top dressing for plants. Vermicomposting offers faster decomposition, higher nutrient content in the resulting compost, and a reduction in the volume of organic waste sent to landfills. It's an excellent option for those with limited space or living in urban environments, allowing them to actively contribute to sustainable waste management while producing a valuable resource for plant growth.

If you're interested in starting a garden, or growing a few things on a windowsill or in a pot, then vermicompost can be an excellent addition to the soil you have. It's also free. Compost can be expensive when you're just starting out on your gardening journey, so having a little extra on a budget is helpful.

The Bokashi Method

The biggest benefit of the Bokashi method is the variety of foods you can compost, such as meat or dairy (which you cannot compost with vermicompost). However, the method needs an outdoor space to put the contents once they're ready. The Bokashi method is a unique and anaerobic composting technique that originates from Japan. Unlike traditional composting methods that rely on aerobic (oxygen-dependent) microorganisms to break down organic matter, Bokashi composting employs a group of specialized anaerobic bacteria to ferment kitchen waste. This method is particularly suitable for urban dwellers or those with limited space if you have a way to dispose of the organic matter once it's ready. There are often initiatives at farmers' markets, local community allotments, and other community-oriented places that will take your compost if you do not have an outdoor space. The Bokashi method is convenient as it can be done indoors and is highly efficient at processing a wide range of organic materials. However, the major drawback is the space required once it's ready for the next stage of decomposition.

The process begins with a Bokashi bin or bucket, which is typically airtight to create an anaerobic environment. These containers are designed with a tight-fitting lid and a drainage system to prevent oxygen from entering. A key component of Bokashi composting is the use of Bokashi bran or inoculant. This bran is infused with a mix of beneficial microorganisms, including lactic acid bacteria, yeast, and phototrophic bacteria. This inoculant kick-starts the fermentation process.

Organic kitchen waste, such as fruit and vegetable scraps, coffee grounds, eggshells, and even small amounts of meat and dairy, are layered into the Bokashi bin. Each layer is sprinkled with a small amount of Bokashi bran. After adding each layer of waste and bran, the contents are compacted to eliminate air pockets, and the bin is sealed tightly. This anaerobic environment promotes the growth of beneficial bacteria that ferment the organic material. The sealed Bokashi bin is left to ferment for about 2 weeks. During this period, the beneficial microorganisms break down the organic matter into a precompost material. The fermentation process is characterized by a pickled or sour smell, which is present only when the bin is open.

Once the fermentation is complete, the precompost material is buried in soil or added to a traditional compost bin. The remaining fermentation liquid, often referred to as Bokashi tea, can be diluted and used as a nutrient-rich liquid fertilizer for plants. The Bokashi method is known for its ability to process a wide variety of food scraps, including those typically avoided in traditional composting. It is a quick and space-efficient way to convert kitchen waste into a valuable soil conditioner. Additionally, because it is an anaerobic process, Bokashi composting produces minimal odors and can be easily managed indoors.

Cold Composting

Cold composting, also known as passive composting or slow composting, is a more relaxed and natural approach to composting organic materials. Unlike hot composting (which we will cover next), which relies on actively managing the compost pile to generate and maintain high temperatures for rapid decomposition, cold composting allows organic matter to decompose at its own pace without the need for regular turning or temperature monitoring. This method is ideal for individuals who prefer a low-maintenance approach to composting or have limited time and resources for active management.

To start cold composting, you begin by collecting organic materials, such as kitchen scraps (fruit and vegetable peels, coffee grounds), yard waste (leaves, grass clippings), and other organic matter (straw, small branches, cardboard). As you accumulate these materials, you can simply add them to your compost pile or bin in layers. Unlike hot composting, there's no strict need for a specific green-to-brown ratio, and the layering process can be less structured. While turning the compost pile is not a requirement in cold composting, it can still be beneficial. Turning the pile occasionally (e.g., every few months) helps aerate the compost and can speed up decomposition to some extent. However, it's not as critical as in hot composting.

It may take several months to over a year for the organic materials to break down completely, depending on factors such as the size of the pile, the types of materials used, and environmental conditions. Eventually, the compost will mature into a dark, crumbly, and earthy-smelling substance that resembles rich garden soil. This indicates that the compost is ready to be used as a valuable soil amendment in your garden or flower beds.

Hot Composting

Hot composting is a method of composting organic matter quickly by creating conditions that promote rapid decomposition. This process involves actively managing the compost pile to achieve higher temperatures, which speeds up the breakdown of materials. Hot composting requires a balanced mix of "green" and "brown" materials. Green materials are rich in nitrogen (such as kitchen scraps, grass clippings, and manure), while brown materials are rich in carbon (such as dry leaves, straw, and wood chips). The compost pile should be large enough to retain heat but small enough to allow air to penetrate to the center. A common recommendation is to start with a pile that is at least 3 feet high (91 cm) and wide. The pile needs to be moist but not wet.

The center of the pile will heat up as the microorganisms break down the material. The temperature can reach between 130°F to 160°F (54°C to 71°C). This heat is essential as it speeds up the decomposition process and kills weed seeds and pathogens. Regularly turning the compost pile is crucial in hot composting. It redistributes heat, moisture, and oxygen, and mixes the materials for more even decomposition. The compost is ready when it's dark, crumbly, and has an earthy smell. The process can take anywhere from a few weeks to a few months, depending on factors such as material composition, pile size, and weather conditions.

Hot composting is effective for producing compost quickly and is especially useful for gardeners who need large amounts of compost. It's also beneficial because the high temperatures can kill harmful bacteria and weed seeds. However, it requires more effort in terms of monitoring and maintenance compared with other methods, such as cold composting.

Local Composting Services

Unfortunately, composting isn't available to everyone, in every city, town or village. And where it is available, it absolutely isn't perfect. You'll find a letter template on page 172 that you can use to write to your local officials to put forward a request for composting services in your area. If you are unsure as to whether composting is available to you, search your local council or governing body's website for compost services.

If your local services are a complete loss, research your local community gardens and farms to see if they will take your compost. Some farmers' markets also will have somewhere for you to bring organic matter and will compost it for you. Another potential option, though this is for those with time, is to potentially start your own community garden. This is a wonderful way to meet people, find a solution for a problem, and build a group of like-minded people.

How to Use Your Homemade Compost in Your Garden

Sending your compost to your local farm is a great way to make use of your compost. An even better way is to bring the food cycle full circle by using your freshly made compost in your home garden. Using homemade compost in your garden is a great way to enrich the soil, promote healthy plant growth, and recycle kitchen and garden waste. The guidelines below can be used as jumping-off points as you learn the ropes. You don't have to stick too rigidly to them. Here's how to use your homemade compost effectively.

Determine the correct time: The best time to add compost to your garden is before planting in the spring or after harvest in the fall. However, it can be added at any time. If your beds are looking a little low or you decide to add some seeds midseason, adding a little compost is absolutely fine.

Test your soil: Before adding compost, it's a good idea to test your soil's pH and nutrient levels. This helps you understand how much compost you need and whether you should balance it with other soil amendments. If you're just getting started in the garden, though, you can skip this step and come back to it at a later date if your plants aren't doing as well as you'd like. In some areas, soil health can be particularly bad, or you may have very acidic soil, which is great for blueberries but not for other plants. This means you'll need to add amendments to balance the soil to provide optimal conditions for your plants to thrive. Amendments may include things such as lime, fertilizer, and organic materials such as compost or manure. Fertilizers tend to vary in nutrients, with a complete fertilizer containing all three primary nutrients: phosphorous, nitrogen, and potassium. For a beginner, I would recommend opting for a fertilizer that contains all three.

Prepare the compost: Make sure your compost is fully decomposed and mature. It should be dark and crumbly and have an earthy smell. If it's still recognizable as the original organic material or smells unpleasant, it needs more time to decompose. If you don't plan on planting immediately, you can always bury the less composed matter at the bottom of the bed. It will continue to break down and enrich the soil over time. But be careful not to plant delicate young seedlings on top of this area.

Mix with soil: Spread the compost over your garden beds and mix it into the top 4 to 6 (10 to 15 cm) inches of soil. For new gardens, a 2- to 3-inch (5 to 8 cm) layer of compost is ideal, mixed into the soil. For established gardens, a 1- to 2-inch (3 to 5 cm) layer is sufficient. This is needed each year to replenish the beds as they sink, and the plants grown will extract many of the nutrients during their growing period.

Use as mulch: You also can use compost as a mulch around plants. This helps retain moisture, suppress weeds, and gradually add nutrients to the soil as it breaks down. This becomes particularly important in the warmer months to help prevent evaporation and negate the need to water as often.

Side-dress plants: Compost can be used to side-dress plants during the growing season. Simply spread a thin layer around the base of the plants. This is especially beneficial for heavy feeders such as tomatoes and can even allow them to grow additional roots and secure themselves through more anchor points.

Mix in potted plants: Mix compost with potting soil for your container plants. A ratio of about 1 part compost to 3 parts potting soil is generally good. You can use this as a start and watch your plants to see how they do. If needed, you can add a little more soil, or compost depending on the health of the plant.

Make compost tea: You can make compost tea by steeping compost in water for a few days and then using the liquid to water your plants. This provides a quick nutrient boost. If you're using the Bokashi method, the bucket will produce tea frequently. This should be heavily diluted in water and then watered into your plants. If the Bokashi tea is not diluted properly, it can burn the roots of your plants as it is quite acidic, so ensure you have about a 1:100 dilution rate. Do not use on foliage and test your tea on less sensitive plants, as they may be able to handle a smaller dilution rate.

Avoid fresh compost for seedlings: Be cautious about using fresh compost around young seedlings, as it can be too strong and potentially damage delicate roots.

Monitor your plants: After applying compost, watch how your plants respond. Good compost should help improve plant vigor and health. If your plants don't respond well, you might need to adjust the amount or type of compost you're using.

The key is to use compost in moderation. Too much compost can lead to nutrient imbalances in your soil. And always continue to add fresh organic material to your compost pile to keep the cycle of nutrients flowing in your garden. As I've said before, gardening is all about experimenting, so make sure to take notes and just try it.

How to Start a Garden

Starting a garden can seem like an incredibly daunting task, especially if you've been inspired by the abundance and success of online home-steaders. I know when I started my first garden, I was overwhelmed by the sheer volume of information online. So, I started small and very optimistically. I went to my local garden center and took note of the seeds on sale. I thought about the foods I eat most often and which would make sense to grow. There's absolutely no point in growing tomatoes if you hate tomatoes or planting several pounds of potatoes if they'll just go bad. So, I started with green peas, a vining plant that does well in most conditions and produces green pods filled with sweet peas. I then moved on to tomatoes and planted several kinds to experiment with which variety would do well. Before I knew it, I was planting seed potatoes, cucumbers, zucchini, blueberry bushes, rhubarb, green beans, and all manner of salad greens. I paid no attention to the rules of spacing or building a functioning trellis. I just threw my gardening hat on and waited patiently to see what would happen. I had many successes and many failures, but with each one I learned something. Plants aren't as fragile as we make them out to be, and many of the rules we garden by are just simply good rules of thumb rather than strict guidelines. I've seen many gardeners evolve their methods over the years through experimentation, so being flexible in your thinking is key.

The best place to start is with what you actually like eating. Write a list of the fruits and vegetables you eat most often throughout the year and when they come into season (if you know). Next, cross-reference this list with what grows well in your area or region and the additional equipment you may need, such as a greenhouse, to improve conditions for certain plants. Don't be put off by this. A greenhouse can range dramatically in price and size and isn't always essential. I don't use a greenhouse because I don't have the space, but I am thinking of building a custom one to fit into a little nook that is otherwise wasted.

The hurdle many of us face is spacing. So, once you've narrowed down your list to the things you like and regional conditions, think about how much space you have to dedicate to your garden. It may be a few pots on a balcony or two raised beds in an old parking space. Whatever it is, however small, you can make something work. Consider a layout that is functional and sketch out your plan ahead of time. Place grow bags or raised beds with a little space in between so you can easily walk through to water, prune, and harvest. (Even for seasoned gardeners, grow bags are helpful. You can move them around, control the quality of the soil, and plant in areas that would otherwise be impossible.)

In my old home, I was lucky enough to have access to a garden at my parents' house with several in-ground raised beds and a conservatory (essentially a greenhouse attached to your house) for the tomatoes and peppers. Once I moved, however, the only real space available was supposed to be a concrete parking space. The ground certainly wasn't optimal, so we worked around this by using grow bags and filling three raised beds with soil, compost, and old twigs from the garden.

Basic Garden Equipment Needs

Everything you need can be found secondhand—at your local community garden, farms, garden nurseries, or with friends and family. I borrowed everything I needed from my family at first, and when I moved, I went straight to the secondhand shop. You would be surprised at the amount of gardening equipment you can get on a small budget. Almost all the pots, seedling trays, and digging tools I bought were found at thrift stores. I also found a soil blocker, which helped to reduce the amount of starter pots I needed and is widely considered a zero-waste tool. The initial investment in your garden can be a little intimidating, but over time you'll find that you can perpetuate your garden each year on next to nothing. Once you have your vermicompost (for example) up and running, you'll have free compost. When you go to harvest your food each season, you'll keep a few aside to dry out and store seeds for next year. You'll find clever and ingenious ways to reuse things in the garden, and over time it will become a self-sustaining ecosystem. Things will become second nature, and your soil health will be through the roof.

Here is the basic equipment that you need:

- Hand trowel
- Soil blocker (optional)
- Trays to hold your seeded soil blocks
- Shovel
- Gardening gloves (essential)
- Pruners (essential)
- Wheelbarrow (if you have a large garden)
- Watering can (size depends on the number of plants you have)
- Twine

If you have a little time and patience, you can easily DIY some pots from old milk cartons, used brown paper, or newspaper and repurpose them as seed starters. I've reused old oat milk cartons for microgreens and starting cucumbers, and they've worked very effectively.

Vertical Gardening

If you are space limited, one of the best ways to get the most out of your garden is to grow vertically. Vertical gardening is a method where plants are grown upward using trellises, stakes, walls, or other support structures rather than spreading out horizontally on the ground. This may look like building a trellis or a triangle for vining plants. It may look like training squash to grow upward rather than trail outward. You may even want to DIY some simple buckets filled with water and nutrients and stack them on top of one another. This approach is especially beneficial in areas with limited space, such as urban environments or small backyards.

By growing plants vertically, you can maximize the use of limited space. This makes vertical gardens ideal for balconies, patios, and even indoor spaces. A wide range of plants can be grown vertically, including various vegetables, fruits, flowers, and ornamental plants. Popular choices include tomatoes, cucumbers, beans, peas, and climbing flowers such as clematis and morning glory.

Vertical gardens use structures such as trellises, nets, cages, wall planters, and hanging baskets to support and encourage upward growth. These structures can be made from various materials, including wood, metal, twine, and plastic. Vertical gardens also can add real beauty to a space. They can be used to create living walls, green facades, and artistic garden displays. Some of the most beautiful examples of vertical gardening I've seen are of walkways completely enclosed by squash and luffa hanging down like ornaments as you pass through.

Vertical gardens can help create microclimates that protect plants from strong winds and intense sunlight. They can also improve air circulation around plants, reducing the risk of disease. If you live in a particularly hot or exposed climate, vertical gardens can be invaluable for water retention and protecting more delicate plants.

For those with mobility issues or difficulty bending, vertical gardens can make gardening more accessible. Raised beds and wall-mounted planters can be positioned at a convenient height for harvesting, pruning, and watering.

Vertical gardening really is a versatile, space-efficient, and aesthetically pleasing way to garden, and it is particularly suited to small or urban spaces. It offers both practical and environmental benefits, making it an essential component to our modern-day gardens.

Start Small and Troubleshoot

Nowadays there is a huge wealth of knowledge online and in print about gardening, from beginners to experts to avid tropical fruit enthusiasts. No matter the amount of space, time, or budget, there is something for everyone. If you're just starting out, a small herb garden is a great place to start. Here's a simple template to get you started.

1. Decide which herbs you use the most and enjoy in your cooking.

2. Thrift a couple of different pots to keep them separate. (Keeping them together is fine, with the exception of mint, which has a habit of completely taking over.)

3. Buy some young plants from a nursery rather than a supermarket, as they tend to be more resilient and this provides an opportunity to support local.

4. Buy a nice potting mix (without peat) and mix with your homemade compost—a 50/50 ratio will work. Then, evenly distribute it among the pots.

5. Give it a good watering, and then dig a little hole and place your herb plants.

6. Cover the roots completely and try to get the soil level with the side of the pot.

7. Water your plants to settle the soil.

8. Place a name tag in the soil to make sure you don't forget what it is you've planted.

9. Prune regularly, just above where two new branches have grown. This encourages your plant to get nice and bushy.

A lot of the time, the trouble comes from overwatering, under- or overfeeding, or simple neglect. Plants are pretty hardy, but it's best to keep an eye on them and create a watering and feeding schedule. This may look like, every Sunday morning, giving each plant a little water, and every other week feeding them with plant food or diluted tea from your Bokashi bin. It's often beneficial to keep a plant diary with any notes that help you to better understand your plants. The last thing you want is for them to die after putting in all that hard work.

Learning to garden takes time and practice, so there's no need to rush and become overwhelmed with hundreds of seedlings when you're just starting out. There are also lots of great forums online with really wonderful communities ready to help you out with answers to your questions. Once you get the hang of growing your own, you'll start to see how important it is where our food comes from and why there are so many ethical considerations to think about. Keeping a conscious kitchen becomes a cycle of sourcing to cooking to reducing waste, and then turning that waste into something useful to allow us to start sourcing our food from our own means. It's no easy feat, but with time it becomes easier to see the system as a whole and where we can do our part.

Completing the Cycle on Your Conscious Kitchen

Throughout this book, it was important to me to present the conscious kitchen with a holistic view—being conscious in the kitchen means starting where you source food, cooking with seasonal ingredients, and composting in the garden to grow the food again. I want you to view this book as a complete cycle, from sourcing your food, to eating seasonally, to composting the scraps. I have presented a lot of information to you in this book, and that can be overwhelming. So, in the spirit of taking small steps and doing what works for you, take out a notepad and write down one thing that resonated with you. Think about how you can begin to apply it in your regular routine. Perhaps you will grow one pot of herbs this year, remember your reusable bags, or get started with vermicompost. Start small and tackle one thing at a time. This book is designed to be picked up again and again, to rejog your memory and to inspire you in times of uncertainty.

My journey into sustainability, cooking, and seasonal eating all stemmed from a change I made one day simply because I wanted to make a better, more conscious choice. I know now that you cannot buy your way out of a crisis, but swapping to using a reusable coffee cup was the catalyst for every decision I've made to live more in line with my values. So, I hope this offers a lesson to you that this isn't an all-or-nothing lifestyle. It's one where we try to make one better decision every day, where we build community and work together to create a better place to live.

Letter Template to Request Composting Services

Feel free to customize this letter with your personal details and any specific concerns or suggestions you have about composting in your area.

[Your Name]

[Your Address]

[City, State, Postal Code]

[Email Address]

[Date]

[Official's Name]

[Title]

[Government Office Address]

[City, State, Postal Code]

Dear [Official's Name],

I am writing to you as a resident of [Your Community/Area] to bring attention to an environmental initiative that could greatly benefit our community: the implementation of local composting services.

As we become increasingly aware of the environmental impact of waste, it is crucial that we explore and adopt sustainable practices. Our community, like many others, generates a significant amount of organic waste that is currently sent to landfills. By introducing a composting program, we can divert this waste from landfills, which not only helps the environment but also can save on waste management costs in the long run.

I understand that implementing a new service can be challenging, but many cities and towns across the country have successfully adopted composting programs. These programs have shown to be beneficial in terms of both environmental impact and community engagement.

Additionally, such a program can be an excellent educational tool for residents of all ages, fostering a greater sense of environmental responsibility and community involvement.

I am eager to support this initiative in any way I can and would appreciate any information you can provide about potential steps forward. Please consider this proposal, and I look forward to your response.

Thank you for your time and attention to this matter.

Sincerely,

[Your Name]

ABOUT THE AUTHOR

Immy Lucas is the creator behind the popular YouTube channel and Instagram handle Sustainably Vegan. Drawn to environmental issues and education since childhood, she has a mission to help and inspire people to live as low impact as possible, from learning how to DIY their own hair products, to shopping unpackaged, to lobbying local government to change. Immy's work is all about finding small ways to alter our behavior over time, using habit change and easy swaps to get there. Her work has been featured in publications such as *Marie Claire*, *The Evening Standard*, and the BBC.

Index